T0197176

SATAN

Still Under Christ's Kingdom's Scrutiny

STEVE C. VARNER

WESTBOW
PRESS®
A DIVISION OF THOMAS NELSON
& ZONDERVAN

WestBow Press books may be ordered through booksellers or by contacting:

WestBow Press
A Division of Thomas Nelson & Zondervan
1663 Liberty Drive
Bloomington, IN 47403
www.westbowpress.com
1 (866) 928-1240

Scripture taken from the King James Version of the Bible.

Edited by Clear Voice Editing.

ISBN: 978-1-9736-6519-9 (sc)
ISBN: 978-1-9736-6518-2 (hc)
ISBN: 978-1-9736-6520-5 (e)

Library of Congress Control Number: 2019907023

Print information available on the last page.

WestBow Press rev. date: 09/28/2019

CONTENTS

1   Satan (Still Under Christ's Kingdom's Scrutiny) 1

2   Satan's Final Attempt, the Power of Betrayal 15

3   Reason for Hope Within 31

4   God's Ticket for Salvation 39

5   Saving by Both Fear and Love from the Second Death 61

6   Things I Learned While Reading the Bible 71

7   The Legend of Epiphany Frost
     (The Controversy of Observing Days) 85

8   When Darkness Reigns 101

9   Dying Spiritually 109

10   Desiring the Fire 121

11   How to Plan a Life 129

12   The One Thing That Both Accuses Me and Defends Me . . . 151

13   Our Reasonable Service 179

14   The Godhead Bodily 189

15   The Hard Things to Understand 193

16   The Irrevocable Calling 203

17   The Time of Testing 209

18   Works Revealed in Fire 217

This book presents a plan to step on Satan's toes in showing the world that it is the Lord Jesus Christ, and He alone, who has the final sting of rebuke. Death brought about by Satan no longer has victory, and physical death has no sting. This is a description of who Satan and his followers really are, the ultimate cowards. It is also a personal and family study guide to understanding God's divine pattern, plan of salvation, why Christians have hope within, and how to teach our children that we are instructed to abhor that which is evil.

1 Corinthians 15:54-55

> [54]The bodies we now have are weak and can die. But they will be changed into bodies that are eternal. Then the Scriptures will come true,

> "Death has lost the battle!
> [55]Where is its victory?
> Where is its sting?"

I always wished that someone would provide me with information that I personally perceived as valuable, and that would help me understand why we have so much chaos in the world. There are a lot of us who would like to understand how to be assured that we are saved. By trying different church congregations and denominations, I found that there are too many man-made creeds and traditions which are not in agreement with the Holy Scriptures. I lost trust in all these so-called religions.

I finally realized through reading that there is one thing definite: I could trust God's Word and His Word only. When God divinely inspired the writers, there was a sound doctrine established which all of them verified in one accord. The principles presented in each book of the Bible provide all the evidence we need to understand God's plan for us.

Now that we have access to the original Aramaic Syriac Peshitta, Greek and Hebrew manuscripts and so many discovered documents it is evident the principles for Salvation handed down by divine inspiration were compiled as an all-inclusive plan, and not picked and chosen at someone's discretion. God told us that as time goes on, our knowledge will increase.

This writing is not intended to be taken solely upon its merit without referencing as many versions of the Holy Bible, Greek lexicons, and concordances as possible while you study. We have been instructed "to seek out our own salvation with fear and trembling." I chose the *King James version* of the Old and New Testament texts available to public domain however I always like to compare Scriptures to the Aramaic Syriac Peshitta which would have been the language Jesus spoke, most likely with Hebrew as well. Since our God is the one who divided the languages I am sure he would know all translations.

I hope this becomes a trustworthy guide to seeking the truth!

PREFACE

Our creator once told a Cherubim angel that he was the seed of perfection, full of wisdom and perfect in beauty; that he was blameless in his ways from the day he was created however, that angel who was on the Holy Mountain decided to rebel, and exaltation was his goal, desiring to be like God. Over the course of time he acquired the names of Lucifer, our relentless opponent, malignant diablo, the slanderer of God's own elect. He became the "prince of this world" and implemented the character of the sin-nature of mankind. He is still called the "god of this age," with his own kingdom, his own throne, and with the power to betray and terrorize. If I am to believe God's Word, I must believe it is a true story. I do believe God's Word as the Truth. The Holy Spirit he gives all Christians is the "Spirit of Truth."

Since his fall from grace he has held in bondage all who are lost and have been rejected from ever seeing Heaven. The Bible says that God did allow him to return and visit Heaven! He was doomed for eternity yet set free for a short time. He is angry because he was cast down from Heaven like a lightning bolt, and he knows his destiny is Sheol, under an everlasting curse with all his demonic angels following him.

Knowing his eternal destination will be the Lake of Fire, he entered the heart of a follower of Jesus, a man named Judas to betray the Son of God. The Son of God, Christ Jesus, who implemented the

Law of Grace and did away with the law of the Old Testament, is the one who provided the way of salvation for all of mankind, the blood atonement for sin.

The power that Satan once had over death was taken away in the resurrection of the Christ from the dead. That power is no longer a victory for him, and no longer has a sting for those who have committed their lives to Christ. Because Jesus is the first born from the dead, you and I can also be resurrected unto life, not damnation, when Christ comes again.

If we do not have the strength or will to resist Satan, he will enter us and dwell, our fate thus becoming humans of disobedience. Through the lust of the flesh, the lust of the eyes, and the pride of life, Satan continues to propagate betrayal and will do so until the Second Coming of the Messiah. Since Satan is condemned, his goal is to take the world with him. He is the mastermind of terrorism!

This book is about what happens when an angel falls from grace. It is "Satan's Final Attempt to Show Off His Power of Betrayal and Terrorism." You can verify all I propose with your Bible (I Peter 5:8, James 4:7).

Satan is still under the scrutiny of all of those who are in God's Kingdom, the Kingdom of Christ.

God shows us His divinely inspired plan! To understand His plan, we must put the Scriptures together into one big picture. He told us to never add nor take away, but to share the principles of His wonderful kindness. There is everlasting value in understanding His awesome words, and they will change our lives forever in eternity.

One of the men Almighty God took up into the heavens (Enoch) has given detailed information that I would encourage all to read, even though it was not recorded in our current Bible.

Genesis 5:21-24

> [21]When Enoch was sixty-five, he had a son named Methuselah,[22] and during the next three hundred years he had more children. Enoch truly loved God,[23-24] and God took him away at the age of three hundred sixty-five.

2 Kings 2:10-12

> [10]"It won't be easy," Elijah answered. "It can happen only if you see me as I am being taken away."[11] Elijah and Elisha were walking along and talking, when suddenly there appeared between them a flaming chariot pulled by fiery horses. Right away, a strong wind took Elijah up into Heaven. [12]Elisha saw this and shouted, "Israel's cavalry and chariots have taken my master away!"[a] After Elijah had gone, Elisha tore his clothes in sorrow.

These are the only two people that we know of whom God took without dying!

Enoch is described as a man who walked with God. Elijah was perhaps the most powerful of God's prophets in the Old Testament. There are also prophecies of Elijah's return (Malachi 4:5-6). I sometimes wonder if it was just a coincidence that Enoch was the seventh from Adam (oh, how He chooses perfect numbers!). This is just a sample of the amazing providence of God.

Of a surety, those experiences had to be awesome for them. The Bible does not specifically say why God did this. Some think they were taken in preparation for a role in the end times, and that they possibly will be the two witnesses in Revelation 11:3-12.

God saved Enoch and Elijah from physical death due to their great faithfulness in serving and obeying Him. Whatever the case, God had His purpose, and while we don't always understand God's plans and purposes, we know that His way is perfect (Psalm 18:30).

If you believe God's Word and you want to know more details of the events that took place in Noah's time, I encourage you to read the book of Enoch, Chapters 6 through 11- of Section II. The Scriptures tell us that knowledge shall increase in the later days, and this is information provided from a godly man whom the Creator had faith enough in to take him without seeing corruption. I personally believe that what he has shared is justified by God Himself.

FOREWORD

While the outcome of this book will ultimately provide perseverance and victory in the heart of the faithful reader, the negative thoughts behind the principle of Satan's power of betrayal and terrorism must be brought to light in a very real and thought-provoking manner. Blame must be placed where it originated, without worrying about stepping on someone's toes, especially Satan's toes. You are encouraged to scrutinize the devil and abhor all he stands for.

My goal is to stand for the cause of God's most holy organization outside of the Body of Christ, the family, as well as those individuals who may not have a blood-line family. Combinations of scriptural evidence and psychological reasoning have been compiled in a manner that can be taught to a child.

I pray that many souls may be saved on Judgment Day by having overcome the deception of the prince of the power of the air of this world, thus hiding a multitude of our sins (James 5:20). We must understand why and how sin entered our world.

You must know that the terror throughout this world is already defeated, and those who are victims have the power to rise and claim victory. My desire is that you will be able to clearly see a path to follow, not because I made it available, but because the character of Christ has made it available in His Word.

This book is dedicated to proving we can and do have hope within us through all the traumatic ramifications of life. There is joy in knowing you have hope.

Satan's final attempt is to bring the world down to his level, the Abyss; he is doomed and doesn't want to go there alone. Proceed with an open mind and you will be blessed. Sow a seed and let God Almighty give the increase. Why is it valuable to read and study about Satan? Understanding where sin originated, and why we struggle with it, is necessary before we can see God's plan to overcome that sin nature.

As you read and study the Scriptures addressed here, hope for light, for you will find it! There is no fear in perfect love. God has given you a spirit of power, of love, and a sound mind, therefore, you can deal with the truth, and the truth will set you free. You don't have to fear any longer!

God's plan for salvation will be discussed in this book. That is why the Apostle Paul told us that there is a pattern of sound words handed down throughout the ages. Refer to 2 Timothy 1:13.

Jesus told John to write to the angel of the Church at Pergamum that He will give them a "white stone" and a new name. Whatever that stone (or gift) is, it must be based upon our obedience to His will.

Reading through the book of 2 Corinthians will help you understand the principle of God reconciling Christ back to Him, and our duty of reconciling others back to God using both fear and love. The key here is that any fear that we portray must be that of reverence of God, not fright of mankind or Satan.

This book addresses additional principles we sometimes don't understand, and that we struggle with. We are not in bondage to any law outside the Law of Grace. I am obligated to keep this teaching in context with the will of God, and I will give an account of everything taught in this writing. The blood Christ shed for His people built a wall of protection against all the evil forces, and nothing can penetrate that wall. We must put up the wall and stand behind it.

Hopefully you will learn to respect the followers of the Kingdom and have patience with them after reading this book.

This writing gives notes related to the three prayers Jesus asked prior to His arrest. He points out the importance of the Holy Spirit in a Christian's life, which is too often forgotten or completely left out of our lives. Also included is a response to the actions of the extremists in this world and their guilt, and why they have so much hatred in their hearts. It is my prayer that all those who have succumbed to the lust of the flesh be snatched away from the leaders of the reprobate.

CHAPTER 1

SATAN (STILL UNDER CHRIST'S KINGDOM'S SCRUTINY)

Satan does two things to those who do not believe that Jesus is the Son of God, that He was born of the Virgin Mary (He came in the flesh), that He died for the sin of the world and rose on the third day and ascended back to Heaven to sit at the right hand of the Creator (the Father), and that He sent the Holy Spirit to those of us who are His true disciples (learners):

1. He blinds (creates a veil) the minds of those who do not believe, and
2. He prevents the light of the Gospel of Christ (the image of God) from shining on those who do not believe.

The deception Satan brings to this Earth is always under the scrutiny of the Body of Christ! When you study your Greek dictionary, you will find that it describes scrutiny like this:

1. A searching examination or investigation; minute inquiry.
2. Surveillance; close and continuous watching or guarding.
3. A close and searching look.

To be on guard for the things that Satan temps us with in his deception, we must learn to resist him, knowing that he is a coward!

James 4:7

> Submit yourselves, then, to God. Resist the devil, and he will flee from you.

The only way these blinded souls can break out of Satan's bondage is by Christians preaching the knowledge of God's glory as we see it in the face of the Lord Jesus.

2 Corinthians 4:1-6 (paraphrased)

> Our ministry is straightforward, and it brings light out of darkness! This is a ministry of the new agreement that God, in His mercy, has given us and nothing will detain us from spreading the good news of exceeding wonderful kindness. We use no magic or clever tricks, no dishonest manipulation of the Bible. We speak the plain truth and so commend ourselves to every man's conscience in the sight of God. If the Gospel of Christ is veiled, the veil has to be in the minds of those who are spiritually dying. The Satanic spirit of this world blinds the minds of those who do not believe and prevents the light of the glorious Gospel of Jesus Christ (the image of God) from shining on them. For it is Christ Jesus the Lord whom we preach, not ourselves; we are your servants for His sake. God, who first ordered light to shine in darkness, has flooded our hearts with His light. We now can enlighten men only because we can give them knowledge of the glory of God, as we see it in the face of Jesus Christ.

So! Who is this spirit of this world who has blinded so many?

Ephesians 2:2

> Wherein in time past ye walked according to the course of this world, according to the prince of the power of the air, *the spirit that now worketh in the children of disobedience:*

Revelation 20:2

> ²And *He laid hold on the dragon, that old serpent, which is the Devil, and Satan,* and bound him a thousand years,

Isaiah 14:12-15

> ¹²How art thou fallen from Heaven, O *Lucifer, son of the morning*! How art thou cut down to the ground, which didst weaken the nations! ¹³For thou hast said in thine heart, I will ascend into Heaven; I will exalt my throne above the stars of God: I will sit also upon the mount of the congregation, in the sides of the north: ¹⁴I will ascend above the heights of the clouds; I will be like the most High. ¹⁵Yet thou shalt be brought down to Hell, to the sides of the pit.

The one who tried to exalt himself to the same position as our Creator has been defeated and is doomed to be driven into the Abyss after a short time of power here on Earth, to deceive and take as many souls with him into the darkness of eternity and forever away from the presence of Almighty God. He has no power over those of us who believe in the Son of God!

John 12:31

> Now is the time for judgment on this world; now *the prince of this world* will be driven out.

John 14:30

> I will not say much more to you, for *the prince of this world* is coming. He has no hold over me.

John 16:11

> And about judgment, because *the prince of this world* now stands condemned.

The spiritually dead are those who are carnally minded instead of spiritually minded.

Romans 8:6

> For to be carnally minded is death; but to be spiritually minded is life and peace.

Romans 8:7

> Because the carnal mind is enmity against God: for it is not subject to the law of God, neither indeed can be.

Romans 6:11

> Likewise reckon ye also yourselves to be dead indeed unto sin, but alive unto God through Jesus Christ our Lord.

I inherited a carnal mind through the sins of Adam and Eve, but in Christ I inherit life eternal and become a new spiritual-minded person. This is called "being made alive" or a "rebirth."

Ephesians 5:5

> For this ye know, that no whoremonger, nor unclean person, nor covetous man, who is an idolater, hath any inheritance in the Kingdom of Christ and of God.

1 Corinthians 15:22

> For as in Adam all die, even so in Christ shall all be made alive.

Jesus Christ (the Word) became flesh and left the glory of Heaven to bring salvation unto all men in form of a man. Once He fulfilled His mission, He returned into His original glory at the right hand of Almighty God and then He sent the Comforter (the Holy Spirit) to guide us as we live our lives in Him.

John 1:1

> In the beginning was the Word, and the Word was with God, and the Word was God. *[the Word became flesh]*

John 1:14

> The Word became flesh and made His dwelling among us. We have seen His glory, the glory of the one and only Son, who came from the Father, full of grace and truth.

Matthew 1:18

> Now the birth of Jesus Christ was on this wise:
> When as His mother Mary was espoused to Joseph,
> before they came together, she was found with child
> of the Holy Ghost.

When Jesus rose from the grave, He promised that He would send another Comforter (other than Himself) to abide with us believers forever. This Comforter is our guide into all righteousness! He reminds us of what Christ told us while He was here on Earth.

John 14:16

> And I will pray the Father, and He shall give you
> another Comforter, that He may abide with you
> forever.

John 14:26

> But the Comforter, which is the Holy Ghost, whom
> the Father will send in my name, He shall teach you
> all things, and bring all things to your remembrance,
> whatsoever I have said unto you.

God the Father, God the Son, and God the Comforter (Holy Spirit) are one in the same being. This is called the Godhead Bodily.

Acts 17:29

> Forasmuch then as we are the offspring of God, we
> ought not to think that the Godhead is like unto
> gold, or silver, or stone, graven by art and man's
> device.

Romans 1:20

> For the invisible things of Him from the creation of
> the world are clearly seen, being understood by the
> things that are made, even His eternal power and
> Godhead; so that they are without excuse.

Colossians 2:9

> For in Him (Jesus) dwelleth all the fullness of the
> Godhead Bodily.

Who could keep our Savior from returning to His original glory after
such exceeding wonderful kindness to redeem us back to His Father?
This was His mission, to give His life for us (become the propitiation
for our sins) and return to His original glory!

When Christ does return the second time, He will gather His chosen
together and we will spend eternity with Him.

Luke 24:26

> Ought not Christ to have suffered these things, and
> to enter His glory?

Romans 3:25

> Whom God hath set forth to be a propitiation
> (sacrifice) through faith in His blood, to declare His
> righteousness for the remission of sins that are past,
> through the forbearance of God.

1 John 2:2

> And He is the propitiation (sacrifice) for our sins: and not for ours only, but also for the sins of the whole world.

1 John 4:10

> Herein is love, not that we loved God, but that He loved us, and sent His Son to be the propitiation (sacrifice) for our sins.

What will Christ do now that He has returned to His glory?

John 14:2

> My Father's house has many rooms; if that were not so, would I have told you that I am going there to prepare a place for you?

John 11:27

> She saith unto him, Yea, Lord: I believe that thou art the Christ, the Son of God, which should come into the world.

It is our duty as Christians to obey the Great Commission given by Jesus Himself (The Great Commission is the Ministry of Reconciliation).

Mark 16:15-16

> [15]He said to them, "Go into the entire world and preach the Gospel to all creation. [16]Whoever believes

and is baptized will be saved, but whoever does not believe will be condemned.

God gave Christ the Ministry of Reconciliation (to lead us back to God) and Christ gave us the same ministry! We all have the same ministry, to lead others from the error of their ways to the truth, in Christ back to Almighty God! (Read 2 Corinthians 5:11 and 18 below.)

God sent His only Begotten Son into the world to redeem us or "buy back" mankind using the blood of Christ. The blood covenant provided by Christ Jesus is the only means of being reconciled back to Almighty God. Jesus' blood was and is the final propitiation for man's sin.

2 Corinthians 5:18

> And all things are of God, who hath reconciled us to Himself by Jesus Christ, and hath given to us the ministry of reconciliation;

2 Corinthians 5:19

> To wit, that God was in Christ, reconciling the world unto Himself, not imputing their trespasses unto them; and hath committed unto us the word of reconciliation.

2 Corinthians 5:11

> Since, then, we know what it is to fear the Lord, we try to persuade others. What we are is plain to God, and I hope it is also plain to your conscience. *[The Ministry of Reconciliation]*

Hebrews 2:17

> Wherefore in all things it behooved Him (Christ) to be made like unto His brethren, that He might be a merciful and faithful high priest in things pertaining to God, to make reconciliation for the sins of the people.

Romans 6:3

> Know ye not, that so many of us as were baptized into Jesus Christ were baptized into His death?

Romans 6:4

> Therefore, we are buried with Him by baptism into death: that like as Christ was raised up from the dead by the glory of the Father, even so we also should walk in newness of life.

Romans 10:6

> But the righteousness which is of faith speaketh on this wise, say not in thine heart, who shall ascend into Heaven? (That is, to bring Christ down from above.)

Romans 10:7

> Or, who shall descend into the deep? (That is, to bring up Christ again from the dead.)

Question: Why should we remind our brothers and sisters in Christ and encourage, admonish, and exhort each other, no matter how unworthy we are? Why would God use such people as me (a

sinner), as the Apostle Paul (who was a murderer), as the woman at the well (an adulteress), to bring our loved ones into remembrance of the ways of Christ?

1 Corinthians 4:17

> For this cause have I sent unto you Timotheus, who is my beloved son, and faithful in the Lord, who shall bring you into remembrance of my ways which be in Christ, as I teach everywhere in every church.

2 Corinthians 10:5

> Casting down imaginations, and every high thing that exalteth itself against the knowledge of God, and bringing into captivity every thought to the obedience of Christ.

Possible answer: Perhaps to bring us into remembrance of the ways Jesus taught, the knowledge of God and to bring our thoughts into captivity to obey His commands.

2 Corinthians 11:13

> For such are false apostles, deceitful workers, transforming themselves into the apostles of Christ.

Matthew 7:15

> Beware of false prophets, which come to you in sheep's clothing, but inwardly they are ravening wolves.

Matthew 24:11

And many false prophets shall rise and shall deceive many.

Matthew 24:24

For there shall arise false Christs and false prophets who shall shew great signs and wonders; insomuch that, if it were possible, they shall deceive the very elect.

Mark 13:22

For false Christs and false prophets shall rise, and shall shew signs and wonders, to seduce, if it were possible, even the elect.

Luke 6:26

Woe unto you, when all men shall speak well of you! For so did their fathers to the false prophets.

2 Peter 2:1

But there were false prophets also among the people, even as there shall be false teachers among you, who privily shall bring in damnable heresies, even denying the Lord that bought them, and bring upon themselves swift destruction.

1 John 4:1

Beloved, believe not every spirit, but try the spirits whether they are of God: because many false prophets are gone out into the world.

This is our reasonable service, to become ministers of the Gospel and renounce our past ways, confess our sins to one another, and become servants to all who are blinded. Those who are not blinded by Satan's veil have the knowledge needed to also fulfill their calling. The choice to serve is ours! If we choose not to acknowledge Christ and who He claims to be, we then are classified as antichrist. And there are many!

2 Corinthians 4:1-6

> Therefore, since through God's mercy we have this ministry, we do not lose heart. [2]Rather, we have renounced secret and shameful ways; we do not use deception, nor do we distort the Word of God. On the contrary, by setting forth the truth plainly we commend ourselves to everyone's conscience in the sight of God. [3]And even if our Gospel is veiled, it is veiled to those who are perishing. [4]The god of this age has blinded the minds of unbelievers, so that they cannot see the light of the Gospel that displays the glory of Christ, who is the image of God. [5]For what we preach are not ourselves, but Jesus Christ as Lord, and ourselves as your servants for Jesus' sake. [6]For God, who said, "Let light shine out of darkness," made His light shine in our hearts to give us the light of the knowledge of God's glory displayed in the face of Christ.

A warning against denying Jesus that Jesus came in the flesh!

1 John 2:18

> Dear children, this is the last hour; and as you have heard that the antichrist is coming, even now many

antichrists have come. This is how we know it is the last hour.

2 John 1:7

I say this because many deceivers, who do not acknowledge Jesus Christ as coming in the flesh, have gone out into the world. Any such person is the deceiver and the antichrist.

CHAPTER 2

SATAN'S FINAL ATTEMPT, THE POWER OF BETRAYAL

The personality of Satan is defined in two divinely inspired writings of Old Testament manuscripts. Satan is described as the evil one in Isaiah 14:12-15, and symbolically as the Prince of Tyrus in Ezekiel 28:12-17. Both writings provide evidence of when the concept of betrayal and terrorism began during the peak of pride in Satan's spirit.

Satan is referred to as the Anointed Cherub that Covereth in Ezekiel 28:14, and God said in the same verse that He (God) was the one who "set him so." God created the cherub, which is a good angelic being, with greater power than man (Hebrews 2:6-7). However, the cherub was not intended to be worshipped (Hebrews 2:5). This angel is described in Ezekiel 10:3-22. Let me shock you into reality! From the very beginning, this was the status of Satan before his great fall from grace.

You ask, "When did this all take place?" To put this into a time frame is very difficult to do; however, I do know what the Bible says about when this happened: that Jesus the man was Jesus (the Word). As we read, in the beginning the Word was with God and was God. The New Testament shows where the Word was manifested in the flesh (the Word became flesh). We also know that Jesus saw Satan fall from Heaven when he exalted himself and gave up the status of a cherubim angel (Luke 10:17-20). At that time, Jesus was the Word, not begotten yet, not in the form of a human being as He was later.

Satan was cast down into the Earth as a serpent on the sixth day, which is also the day that man was created. You can read that in the book of Genesis.

So, we know that Satan was cast down from Heaven long before God implanted the seed into the Virgin Mary and brought Jesus the man (the Word) into the world. Jesus came to destroy the power Satan gained as the prince of the power of the air here on Earth. Jesus came to destroy death as we know it in the physical body. Jesus came to give life and more abundantly, exceeding above and beyond we can imagine if we believe Him.

One of the offices of the cherub was to wait on God. This is the meaning of "The Anointed Cherub that Covereth". So, before Satan's fall from grace he was assigned to wait upon his creator.

Some of the angels were sent forth to announce God's law. Acts 7:53 states that "the law was received by the character of angels." To paraphrase, Hebrews 2:2 says, "If the message spoken by angels was a mandate and all transgression, unforgivable sin, and blatant disobedience was given justifiable reward," how will we today escape that same judgment by ignoring the salvation plan given in the New Testament?

Luke 1:18

> God's message was to be conveyed by both Cherubim
> and Seraphim angels.

The angels were ordained to protect God's people. The story of Lot being pursued by angels in the morning saying, "Get up and take your wife and your two daughters who are here, before you are consumed in the iniquity of the city" is a good example. I encourage you to read this scenario (Genesis 11:27; 12:1-13; 18:16-19, and 38).

The angels were ordered to inflict divine penalties on behalf of Almighty God: "Let the people be like the husk blowing in the wind and let the angel of the Lord discipline them." "Let their path be like the darkness of the Abyss, and treacherous, and let the angel of Jesus be the one to persecute them" (Psalms 35:5-6; 2 Samuel 24:16; I Chronicles 21:14-17). Perhaps Satan liked this power so much that he let it overwhelm him into the acts that followed. It is true even today; once we have been given power to accomplish many things by God, we soon find ourselves wanting more power.

The angels were ministering spirits. "For God will place His angels in charge over you to keep you sound in the ways of judgment." "They will guide your feet and keep you from kicking against the stones" (Psalms 91:11-12; Hebrews 1:13-14). We can see here that the responsibilities given by God to the angels were many and diverse, to the extremes.

The good angels guarded cities and even nations while sharing in the counsel. The New Testament writers said they would confirm that there is joy in the presence of the angels of God over any sinner willing to change (Luke 15:10). In recompensing the House of Israel, in chapters 9 and 10 of Ezekiel, verification is made that there indeed was life and spirit in the cherubim, as mentioned in Ezekiel 10:17-22.

Out of the acts of betrayal of God's plan (when Satan entered in) came the necessity of sanctification. God was betrayed by His chosen race, Israel, and declared execution of judgment on the nation for the remaining children of that race to be sanctified. The remnant that was preserved would ultimately carry on the chosen race lineage through the Melchizedekian bloodline, 1 Corinthians 6:11: "And some of you, before accepting Christ as your Savior were carnal minded or materialistic, but now you are washed in the blood and are sanctified and justified in the Lord Jesus Christ and by the spirit of our God."

God's plan now was to send the Word, a part of His triune Godhead, the Christ, to Earth in the form of man to redeem or buy back all of those who would submit to Him. He also sent the third part of His Godhead, the Holy Spirit, or Comforter, as a gift to all of those who obeyed His commandments. Therefore, God said in Genesis 1:26, "Let us "the Godhead Bodily" make man in our image and likeness because we are created in the image of the Father, the (Word) Son, and the Holy Spirit." Today, this is called the Trinity, Triune Godhead or the Godhead Bodily.

This is where the concept of the Trinity came to be. God is three personalities in one: The Father, the Son, and the Holy Spirit. The Scriptures also teach that the Word was from the beginning, which means that this character (the Christ or Messiah) existed even before Christ appeared on Earth as a man. Don't let it confuse you, even if it is hard to understand right now.

There truly are no contradictions in the Bible if we look hard enough. God will make His dwelling place in the hearts and minds of those who are obedient to His will. We (Christians) are the temple or dwelling place of Almighty God's Holy Spirit. Christ lives in us and He is our hope of sharing in God's glory. There are many I work with who believe we as Christians believe in 3 Gods. This is not the case at all! One brother put it this way; water can be liquid, it can be steam and it can be ice. It is still water, just 3 different characteristics of the same element.

The power of betrayal, deception, and terrorism continues. The day Satan was cast down into the Earth as a serpent, the sixth day, is also the day that man was created. On the seventh day God told Adam to name the animals, so Adam named the serpent, which was Satan, in the cast-down form. After creating woman for Adam, as a helper suitable for him, the serpent immediately brought about betrayal in the form of beguilement. Here he calls God a liar: "Ye shall not surely die as God has warned you." Adam and Eve believed a lie over the One who had created them. Satan did not let any grass grow under his belly! Now mankind was afraid, naked, and they hid from Almighty God (Genesis 3:4). This is the beginning of terrorism.

This is where the serpent is cursed (Genesis 3:14) above all other animals. As far as our betrayal of God in this event, the woman receives great sorrow and pain in childbirth, as well as a focused desire to her husband and submission under his rule (Genesis 3:16). For Adam's betrayal of God, the ground became cursed and he would eat of it in sorrow all the days of his life, and would live among the thorns and thistles, and would eat the herb of the field: "in the sweat of his face would he labor for food" Genesis 3:17-19.

God cast out Adam and Eve from the Garden for their betrayal, just as He did Satan from Heaven. The act of betrayal can only lead to a casting-out from the place we resided while in God's grace. Now, neither Satan nor mankind are in God Almighty's grace. It is interesting to note what God placed at the east end of the garden, to keep the way of the Tree of Life: "Cherubim and a flaming sword which turned every way." Yes, good angels.

Revelation 8:6

> The apocalyptic trumpets will be raised in sound by
> the good Angels.

Matthew 24:31, Mark 13:27

> The good angels will gather God's elect people for
> the judgment day.

Freedom of choice was not withheld from the angels, nor is it withheld from us today. God is unchanging. He offered all His creation the right to make choices and to show appreciation for His wonderful kindness in the gift of life or blaspheme His holy name in denial. It was outright selfishness and rebellion on Satan's part to exalt himself above his creator.

He was known throughout the Bible as Satan, Lucifer, the seal of perfection, full of wisdom and perfect beauty, blameless, adversary, relentless opponent, enemy, like a roaring lion, accuser, angel of light, the dragon, slanderer, murderer and liar, father of lies, deceiver, prince of the world, god of the ages, prince of the power of the air, malignant diablo, and was referenced as the Prince of Tyrus. *So! Why would the divinely inspired writers of this book, called the Holy Bible, use so many names to refer to one being? Because he is the "master of deception" and puts on so many false faces? From a good angel to a murderer! How diverse can one get?*

Ezekiel 28:1-2

> The Word of the Lord came again unto me saying, Son of Man, say to the Prince of Tyrus, the Lord God will do this; because your heart is exalted by yourself and you said that you were God and sat in His seating the mist of the seas (*addressing the Prince of Tyrus*). But you're just a man and not Almighty God. Even though you let your heart believe that you are God. (*Compare this with the 14th chapter of Isaiah*).

Ezekiel 28:16

> I the true God will destroy you, O covering cherub (angel), from the middle of the stones of fire.

The Lord God almighty even confronted Satan and made the statement that "at one time even he was perfect in all of his ways."

Ezekiel 28:15

> You were perfect in all your ways from the day I
> created you and then through your own deceitfulness
> and pride, iniquity was found in you.

He, Lucifer, will be thrown into the Lake of Fire (Revelation 20:10).
His temporary dwelling place is the Earth (Job 1:7).

Rev. 12:12

> I paraphrased this scripture as follows; "Beware
> all of you inhabitants of the Earth and of the sea!
> For the fallen angel who is now called Satan will
> come down to you and bring his deception and great
> wrath to devour you because he knows now he does
> not have a long time here as the prince of the power
> of the air to take as many souls as possible into the
> Lake of Fire when he goes".

He has been allowed access back into Heaven since his original
casting out, as recorded in Job 1:6. Remember, though, that he does
not have the power in Heaven that he has here on Earth. He is the
prince of the power of the air, and not Heaven. He is a condemned
loser!

The most intriguing question which we derive from God's Word is
sometimes hard to explain. Why did Eve betray God in the Garden?
Why did Adam fall to her enticement, therefore betraying God's
will as well?

The serpent is the creator of the sin nature, of which both Adam and
Eve became victim. Satan denied what God had told both would
happen if they disobeyed His command. The sin nature of Satan

from the very beginning has convinced man that "God was a liar," and that "Eve would not surely die." However, he beguiled her to believe she would be opened to new knowledge: "Be like God," and thus know the difference between good and evil. In her desire to become wise and soak in pleasure she gave in to sin, to disbelief, and convinced Adam to do the same.

Genesis 3:1-6

> Satan had, and continues to have, that same master craftsmanship to deceive, to implant wickedness and evil purpose in our minds, to pull us from grace, to enter our being and control us. He is active in his craft today.

He can cause sickness and suffering (Acts 10:38; 1 Timothy 3:7). He has the power of death (Hebrews 2:14). And for those without Christ, he is "the victor over the grave." Without the resurrection of Jesus Christ on the third day, there would be no hope. We must fight to maintain an understanding of God's plan or Satan will rob us of our salvation (Mark 4:15).

In all this deception, we need to remember the salvation that came. Christ's authority, his death, burial and resurrection are the only thing's that seals the doom of Satan (Isaiah 14:15; Revelations 12:10).

It is a good place to stop and remind ourselves that Satan is the one under the curse, which has no ending. Our curse, which is temporary and of a carnal nature (sin), can be overcome through commitment to the cause of Christ and only that. Obedience to God's will! Faith!

This powerhouse of betrayal, in his last attempt to gather souls, along with his angels (Revelations 12:7-10), has no chance of surviving eternal damnation. He will be tormented day and night forever and ever (Revelation 20:10; James 4:7; and I Peter 5:8).

We can have victory in all this confusion and demoralized cultures that stems from that initial act of exaltation. That promise (the right to become children of God) was implemented in the resurrection of Christ from the dead (Ephesians 1:19-23). We can be free! (Acts 26:18; Matthew 4:1-11; Romans 5:12-19; 1 John 3:8; Colossians 2:15; Hebrews 2:14-15; Ephesians 2:4-6; Hebrews 1:13; 1 Peter 3:22; Luke 10:17-20; 2 Corinthians 4:4; Ephesians 2:1-3; Colossians 1:13; Ephesians 4:27)

Are we ignoring the power of betrayal that Satan so cunningly and falsely made acceptable today, such as disrespect of parents, homosexuality, **reprobate** marriage lifestyles, alternative incestuous behavior, and abuse, infidelity in marriage, occultism, demonology, materialism, and ungodly acceptable vocabulary? Are we ignorant of his power and working, or are we afraid to speak out, to teach the truth fearing we may step on someone's toes?

Why? Do we feel that stepping on Satan's toes may put us in a position for spiritual failure? Could it be that we are so weak we are afraid of what man may do to us?

The Bible teaches us to "fear not him that can kill the body, but to reverence the one (Almighty God) who can both destroy our bodies and send us to Hell." God is a jealous God and He does not think it wrong to place judgment on those who do not accept His exceeding wonderful kindness and redeeming mentality. There will be a resurrection unto life eternal at the same time a resurrection unto damnation.

Deuteronomy 4:24

For the Lord your **God** is a consuming fire, a **jealous God**. (this has been revealed 12 times in the Holy Scriptures)

I contest that our duty is to fear God and keep His commandments, and to "abhor that which is evil." If we worry what may happen to us in speaking out against Satan, we truly have no place in God's graces (exceeding wonderful kindness). That would be like a Christian saying he believes in God and Jesus; however, he has some question as to the necessity of the Holy Spirit in his life. He simply does not believe the Scriptures! Jesus said it plain and simple: "I will send you another Comforter, the Holy Spirit, to guide you into all righteousness." There is no fear in "perfect love." God is love, and Christ is love! If we want to eliminate fear, we must without exception open our hearts to winning back our families and the lost, and taking that which is ours, for Christ! We must be followers, not just fans!

If I do not take advantage of my God-given ability, my talent to reach the lost, to occupy my mind with the Gospel, then I am committing spiritual suicide and taking my loved ones with me! If I can lead one person from the error of his ways, then I have hidden a multitude of sins, both theirs and my own sins as well (James 5:20). This single verse of scripture must be one of the most rewarding statements in the New Testament! Please take the time to read it for yourself. This one scripture tells us how valuable one soul is to God. This one scripture describes how much you are loved by God.

If our God is willing to hide a multitude of sins for leading one soul from the error of his or her ways, why would we not listen and try to do it? I cannot ignore this opportunity! I must revere God Almighty because He has the power and is kind enough to save me. I must not fear Satan! However, be aware of His awesome power! Remember he is the defeated. I cannot become preoccupied with any exalting of Satan in our society, whether through movies, media, news, alternative lifestyles, etc. He is evil, and I must hate that which is evil and not fear what he may do to me!

The mindset of every reader here should be to see the Lord Jesus Christ as the center of life and existence. Keep Christ in focus, and Satan under constant scrutiny, as the motive to press on.

I would like to tell a story about what happened to me in a pipeline camp in Alaska back in the mid-70s. I was staying in a camp in a place called Happy Valley. My stay was short, and not a lot of memories of that period are in my mind. I will suffice the experience to be shared in a poem I wrote specifically about my roommate, who I later found out was an upper echelon warlock. I was told about his death by a friend of his who was in a truck accident with him when he died.

His friend was also hurt very badly, and I met him in the airport in Fairbanks on my R&R. He told me that my roommate had been killed in a head-on collision with a pipe-hauling truck, and that his own mother and father would not go to his funeral because there were more than 500 witches and warlocks in attendance. This has reminded me all the years since that Satan really is active, and he truly is aware of Jesus. The short time I shared a bunkhouse with this person, he would never stay in the room when I was there.

The first thing I did when I unloaded my bags was to lay my Bible on the stand between us. However, being a weak Christian and quiet-spoken, I did not attempt to discuss religion with him. I never said a derogatory word to him. The only time he spoke to me was when he left after I came into the room; he always left candles burning above his bed, and all I remember him saying was, "Don't blow my candles out." I don't remember ever hearing any other words from him. This is the poem I wrote:

The walls
What did the warlock do to my being,
now that he's dead and gone
Did the spell cease at his dying,
will the ramifications go on
Where are the lost years,
was that part of it all,

did my senses cease to be
Could it be that he brought about the fall,
now can I ever see
Could a candle have been whispered out
from the shutting of our door
And cause the death he fated
and tied us to the floor
I'm not convinced I faltered
although they come and go
They make me feel as if I'm haltered,
cause blessings not to flow
He must have called a legion,
one for each passing day
He blamed me for something;
surely I stood in his way
In laughter one lay dying,
just to rise again
I watched us from the ceiling,
Fulfilling his entire plan
They too are so powerless,
yet deceiving eyes they strain
They take from me my loved ones,
but can't bind me with their slings
They desire to snatch
for the tomb reserved for fire
I fight each waking hour,
drink faith before it grows sour
Greater is He within me
than he who sent the demons
My Savior guides eternally
as Satan spews his semen
I know he would
to win my soul,
Degrade my heart in shame
He hates the very core of words

spoke in Jesus' name
Upper echelon
he might have been,
his candle was blown out
Not by breath I focused on,
but God's Word snuffed! No doubt!
My Bible lay between us,
the flames above his bed
My silence
when he entered,
heaped coals upon his head
They said
his wake was an awesome sight,
cathedral full of robes
Worshiping their master,
lawless,
fully clothed
Headlong he died in mountains
a gruesome scene I'm sure
The demons must have cried aloud
when Satan lost his lure
Though they come
and visit me often,
they cannot touch my self
Just as their master trembled
they too, must fear my wealth
Now they've aimed and wounded
by the piercing through my heart
By blinding,
by stealing
to rip my world apart
I may shed the tears of sorrow
in moments short and passing
But the demons too
have lost tomorrow,

for my life is everlasting
Consume they may
in bits and pieces,
the edges of my soul
But my sword is sharper,
for you see
"The blood has made me whole"
I wish I could have stood
before his body
and boldly proclaimed
That the power of his candles
could not stand
against Christ name
The crowd would have killed me
True!
but maybe one would see!
Their master was a coward
when God's Word was found in me
The warlock only showed his face
a time
or maybe two
Three weeks in pure damnation,
he knew soon he would be through
With all of his deception
he knew his time he'd lost
God's Word lay in between us,
surely now he'd pay the cost
He had led so many down before
to hell's dark holding place
Until he saw my Lord's impression in my face
Stronger love abides in me,
for not wavering
even in fear
And housing beside Satan,
slumbering so near

Each day the demons hang around,
they in awe too fear their fate
Summoned up to pressure me
and make me succumb
before my dying day
The power that's within me
will snatch the one's they've seized
They cry in anguish
because they too
in "Messiah" truly believe
They're lost forever,
the master cannot revive,
and their souls are sealed in fate
They cannot love,
redeem the victory,
nor overcome their burning hate
As I remember the candles,
no fear did cross my eyes
My teaching of one in sandals said
"look far, far beyond the bluest skies"
To a place where no man has seen,
I found the substance in
The walls the blood of Jesus built
bound the warlock,
my soul, he could he could not win

If you asked me if I believe Satan is alive and active today, I would say *absolutely*. If you asked me if I believe that Satan's demons are active, and that they also believe in and tremble at the name of Jesus, I would say *most definitely*. If you asked me if I believe there is suffering for Christians today as there was in Biblical times, I would say *yes*! Satan has tried to steal my joy! I still struggle with keeping it!

The acts of terror we see every day throughout the world are committed by the cowards called antichrist. Is it hard to live the

Christian life? It is the most difficult thing I have ever done. If you asked me why I keep trying to proclaim Christianity and scrutinize Satan, it is because I have a reason for the hope that is within me, even though I am not worthy to be called a child of God! I will continue to pray for mercy, grace, wisdom and knowledge with understanding because I really want to share in God's glory one day! How awesome will it be to know the power of resurrection? Almighty God has answered so many of my prayers, and still does. The next chapter will give you more specific reasons I have that hope.

When God brought Jesus, His firstborn Son, into the world, He commanded all His angels to worship Him. And when God speaks about the angels He says, "I change my angels into wind and my servants into flaming fire" (Hebrews 1:6-7). My desire is to become a flaming fire for my Creator.

CHAPTER 3

REASON FOR HOPE WITHIN

Of all the haunting scriptures that pop up in my mind, there is one that keeps coming back repeatedly:

1 Peter 3:15

> Always be ready and willing to give a reason of the hope that is inside me.

How in the world can I answer a question like that? Have you ever had that problem with the things you were taught as a child, because you never quite figured out how to uphold the teaching or commandment such as this one?

I urge you to keep searching for answers. Usually they can be found in the same place and from the same person that the instruction came from. Let's look at a few!

Uncle Walter used to say from the pulpit all the time, "Don't take my word for it, get your Bible out and read it." I concur, verify what I am saying is true! Never take a preacher's word without confirming it in the Bible.

Colossians 1:27

> Christ in you is your Hope of Glory.

At least there are some scriptures that give direct answers to this question. Christ personality must be inside me for Him to be my hope in glory, so I'd better get His thoughts and character inside me if I am going to have any hope of glory after this life is over. There are specific directions in the Word of God telling me how to get Christ in me. We will address these specifics for God's plan to work in our life later.

All that you have ever hoped and dreamed Heaven would be like will be revealed and you will be an incorruptible being to enjoy it and worship God for ever and ever. So don't faint, whatever you do.

Colossians 1:5

> The Son is the image of the invisible God, the firstborn over all creation.

The word of the truth of the Gospel proclaims that the hope that is laid up for you in Heaven is indeed secure and available right now. You and I don't have to see all the things we hope for with our naked eyes right now.

Does this mean I have no hope while I am here on Earth? Do I have to die and go to Heaven before I can have hope? Is the only place I can hear about hope found in the truth of the Gospel? These are a lot of questions, huh? The following scriptures will help us understand these questions. The previous one just answered a lot of them. If Christ is in me here on Earth, then I can hope for whatever is in Heaven when I get there, right? So yes! I do have hope while here on Earth if Christ is dwelling in me. The faith I have in Christ is the substance of all things I hope for. My faith is also is my evidence of the things which I cannot see while I am here on Earth. I can only read about how wonderful a heavenly dwelling place might be right now, because I have never seen it with my own eyes. No! I don't have to die before I can experience hope. And yes! The only place I can hear about true hope is in the Gospel, the written word of God. Any other books or manmade creeds can give false hope and non-true statements if not based on the divinely inspired word of God. That is why I avoid creed books. They are man-made and not necessarily divinely inspired.

Psalm 42:11

> Why are you so down and out, my soul? And why
> are you upset with me inside? Hope in God and give
> Him who is the health of my countenance, and my
> God all the praise.

There is a cure for being depressed and not having anything positive to say when it comes to hope. All the acts of violence in our world make it stressful, depressing and often oppressive to live and work today.

You can and should be ready to give an answer to anyone who asks that you do have hope, and your hope is in your God, your Creator, and you will live with Him and His children for eternity. You have a reason now to lift your head up from the oppression and depression Satan creates within all of us (remember, that is his goal). God said I have given you a spirit of power, of love, and of a sound mind, not fear! We just need to be reminded daily that God does love us and can heal of us of being down and out.

1 Peter 1:21

> There are those who believe in God that raised Jesus
> from the dead and gave Him glory that our faith and
> hope might be in God.

Jesus received all the glory in His ministry, His death, His burial and resurrection from the dead, and His ascension, and by Him we believe in an Almighty God. God is the one who raised Jesus up from the dead and took Him from this Earth back into Heaven where He started on His journey of reconciliation. We are told that we too can share in a place without death and be beside our God and Savior for eternity. This is a reason for the hope within us.

1 Peter 1:13 *(the definition of resiliency, resolution, and reverence for Almighty God)*

> All of you gird up the loins of your mind, be sober minded, and hope to the end of this age when at the Revelation of Jesus will hand you that which you have hoped for in a vivid physical and spiritual way. Your mansion, your freedom from sickness and death and tears and no night there!

Wow!

What a mouthful of stuff! God is telling me whatever I do regarding hope, I must do it unto the end. That means to just keeping on keeping on and don't faint, don't quit, don't give up! I must hope for grace (such wonderful kindness) when Jesus comes back to get us and take us into Heaven. That is a pretty good reason to hope that Jesus has mercy and forgiveness for all the weakness I have, and that no matter what I have done I can still make eternity and live instead of dying spiritually. This flesh isn't the end of this life.

Psalm 31:24

> All of you that hope in the Lord be of good cheer and rejoice. Don't express your faith in weakness. You have been given a spirit of truth, love and sound mind, not fear.

I don't have to have a weak heart. I can overcome being downtrodden when Satan has overcome me through his deception and violence. Hope in a Savior is worth being happy for, and one thing I learned is that if I let him, Satan will steal my joy for sure. The hardest thing for me to overcome is not expressing my faith in weakness. That is why I put my feelings in writing; I have a hard time vocalizing them.

1 John 3:3

> And if you have this hopeful attitude you will also
> purify yourself even as Christ is pure.

This same Bible that says "all have sinned and fallen short of the Glory which is in Christ Jesus" tells me that my hope will clean me up to the point that I can be accepted as I am? Dirty! Yet clean, presented white to God on Judgment Day. We all must work at accepting such an offer because we are carnal-minded, and to get a grip on what Jesus has offered is sometimes inconceivable.

For most of us this concept is very hard to get a grip on! That is why it is called hope. That is why it is directly related to grace (unmerited favor), or God's overwhelming kindness. I can be something I am not physically in Christ, simply because He said I could. The biggest chore I have is to believe what Christ said. That is truly something to hope for, knowing I can never be what I would like to be for my Savior, but I am presented to God by Christ as if though I had never sinned. When I fully understand this concept and don't reject it, then I have a reason for the hope that is within me. What an awesome reason.

Proverbs 14:32

> The wicked person is driven away in his wickedness:
> but the righteous ones will have hope in both his
> physical death and the spiritual *(second death)*.

The second death, as talked about in Revelation 21:4-8, is what our hope keeps us from experiencing. So those who are wicked in this world will not escape eternal damnation, their part in the Lake of Fire that burns with fire and brimstone.

He that overcomes shall inherit all things. He that is fearful and unbelieving, and the abominable, and murderers, and whoremongers, and sorcerers, and idolaters, and all liars shall have their part in the second death. I don't have to worry about dying the second death because I have a reason for the hope that is within me. What a blessing to have such hope. I will experience the first death, the physical body going back to the dirt, just as all people will.

The second (spiritual) death could be explained as the final abiding place where the unbeliever's soul spends eternity.

There are no more chances at that point to change my destiny, so being prepared when it comes time to leave my physical body is very important. The plan God set forth includes two paths: one wide path, and it is very broad, and many people will enter it; and the other is straight and narrow, and few there are that will ever find it.

1 Peter 1:3

> Blessed be the God and Father of Jesus Christ our Lord and Savior, which according to His exceedingly abundant mercy hath begotten us again unto a hope which is alive by the resurrection of Jesus Christ from the Dead.

If you asked me to give you a reason for the hope that is within me, I would have to quote this scripture. I have been begotten again (given a second chance, quickened), or maybe been given a second birth, so to speak. Purely out of mercy from my Creator I have been given the opportunity to make God happy by trusting and believing in what He says!

Jesus, who before the world was a "Word spoken," an all-knowing, all-seeing powerful Creator who existed in the form of three personalities: God the Father, Son (Word), and Holy Spirit. The Word was with God and the Word was God. "For God is a spirit and he who worships Him must worship Him in spirit and in truth." "He who has believed on me has believed also on the Father, for I and the Father are one." (John 16:13; John 14:16-17; John 7:38; Isaiah 59:21; Luke 11:13; John 4:14; Ezekiel 36:27; Galatians 3:14; Romans 8:26-27; Romans 4:17; Romans 8:15)

This is the reason for the hope that is within me. There are only two things in our life that direct us to the point of eternal abiding places: one is truth, the other is error.

Jesus has told us there is no riding on the fence; we must be on one side or the other. In other words, He told us if we are lukewarm He will spew us out of His mouth. So, we must be either hot or cold. Living in truth or living in error.

Psalm 71:5

> For you are my Hope, O God and you are my trust
> from my youth.

We all need someone we can trust. From the time we are born up to the age of accountability, we have our mom and dad to protect us. Once we are old enough to understand right from wrong, we understand that there is a target to aim for and must give an account for wrongdoing. Once we understand what faith is, and become accountable for our sins, we then need to be taught a moral foundation. This is the need to have hope! The need to have faith in someone or something is in every human being. God had a big plan and He wants you to be part of it. He asks you to trust in Him and His plan and can give the reason for the hope that is within you.

His son Christ Jesus is the reason. He was an all-inclusive gift which replaced the older plans God set forth in the patriarchal and Mosaic dispensations (ages, laws). Jesus is the center of the last dispensation of grace as we know it today; there will not be another plan (law) by God because Christ was the ultimate sacrifice. Only His blood could make God happy. The Old Testament Law of Moses was just the schoolmaster to get us to the point where Christ's blood atonement was enough for God to redeem us. The other plans were never good enough, and Jesus told God that now He was going to be the one to provide the happiness to God that He didn't get through the sacrifices of bulls and goats in the older days. There is no need for any more sacrifice because the ultimate sacrifice has been made.

Ephesians 2:14-15

> Christ gave His own body to destroy the Law of Moses with all its rules and commands.

Colossians 1:25-27

> If I will allow Christ to live in me I am guaranteed that I will someday share in God Almighty's wondrous glory!

This is the whole mystery of the New Testament as Paul told the Gentiles. This is the complete message. For ages and ages, it was kept secret from everyone, but now it should be your reason for hope that is within you. If you follow God's plan of salvation, you will share in His glory. All the worldly sacrifices and suffering we must endure here on Earth are nothing to acquire sharing in God's glory one day. We just must not faint getting to that place. Sure, there will be those sacrifices and losses in life! I have experienced them as well but remember "not fainting" is the key to living a successful Christian life.

CHAPTER 4

GOD'S TICKET FOR SALVATION

Hearing
Believing
Repentance
Confession
Baptism
Obedience
Faith
Hope
Love
Prayer
Works
The Gift of the Comforter
Communion with Christ

When the actions of hearing, believing, repentance, confession, baptism and obedience have taken place in our life, we are guaranteed a home in Heaven. These acts also require other works to prove our faith. The works do not save us, they only determine the reward we are granted in the judgement day. The wonderful grace of Almighty God is what saves us. These acts of faith in the blood shed by Christ on the cross will sanctify us in that wonderful gift of kindness. This faith is the substance of the things we hope for in Christ. It is the evidence of the things we cannot see here on Earth, but only dream of. Only then can we add to our faith by prayer, a life of virtue, temperance, patience and godliness, with brotherly kindness. We show our faith by our works to prove that our faith is not a dead faith. Our works will ultimately be tried by fire, and when tried, if they remain, we will receive that place prepared for us in Heaven. (If is always a big word. It implies that there are conditions, requirements or stipulations on which outcomes depend.)

HEARING

Romans 3:23, 10:17

The only way we can ever establish faith in this world is to be able to call upon the One who created us. But how can we call upon the One who made us if we don't believe in a supernatural being? We must believe that He exists.

How can we believe in a God this powerful if we have never heard the story of creation? Someone must preach this good news, and God must send them out to proclaim the message. The whole chapter of Romans 10 testifies that indeed this good news has been spread throughout the whole world, so the world has heard about the wonderful kindness of God.

John 6:45

Jesus himself said "it is written in the prophets, and they shall be all taught of God. Every man therefore that hath heard, and hath learned of the Father, cometh unto me." He goes on to say, "He that believes on me shall have everlasting life."

BELIEVING

So, what are we supposed to believe in? John 6:45 says we are to believe that Jesus is who He said He was: the only begotten Son of God, and God in the flesh.

Matthew. 1:21

So! What is the good news? Verse 21 says "and Mary shall bring forth a son and you are commanded to call His name Jesus because He will save His people from their sins." This is the principle of grace, or wonderful kindness.

The principle of the gift of grace is the wonderful kindness God gave us when He chose to send Himself to Earth in the form of a Messiah, a man called Jesus. Jesus is the third character of the Godhead Bodily. God the Father and the Holy Spirit are the other characters in the Godhead.

Grace is simply the act of granting someone or something favor when it is not merited or deserved. We live in a dispensation, or age of grace, as mentioned in Ephesians 3:2. This gift was given by one man, as read in Romans 5:15. We are justified in God's eyes by this grace, and through Jesus Christ, which is verified in Romans 3:24. Grace is what we should pray for, as was prayed for by the Biblical disciples (1 Corinthians 16:20).

Acts 19:1-5

Without grace there would be no plan of salvation!

Read Ephesians 2:8 in any version of the Holy Bible.

Grace was not given under the Mosaic Law or in Old Testament time. It only came when Christ was given to us by God, and when we received the truth as shown in 1 John 1:17.

We get strength when we accept or believe in the principle of grace (2 Timothy 2:1).

The concept of grace is the only means by which we obtain our salvation. When we are obedient to the cause of kindness through Christ being offered as a sacrifice, we will obtain our home in Heaven (2 Corinthians 12:9).

We have all been subjected to the concept of grace in one way or another. It teaches us to deny ungodliness and worldly lust, and that we should live to the best of our ability while we are here on Earth (Titus 2:11-12).

The gift of grace is only at our disposal if we are humble enough to accept it (1 Peter 5:5, 10 and 12). Through grace, in association with a short time of suffering and accepting of God's gift, we have a way to grow unto perfection and to be strengthened in the heavenly Kingdom and establish a place in the lamb's Book of Life.

REPENTANCE

Jesus told us that the daily events we experience in life do not determine our surviving spiritually. Just because accidents and illness happen to some, and others never experience such traumatic events, does not mean that one person's sins have been greater, so God decides to be angry at them. We are all required to repent or face everlasting punishment on Judgment Day (Luke 13:3).

There was a time when God would just wink at us in our ignorance, but now He commands all men to change their ways, because we are His offspring and He alone has established the boundary in which we have our habitation.

CONFESSION

Romans 10:9-10

My heart's desire is that you may be saved. So have zeal of God, but not according to knowledge. There is an end to the law of righteousness, and it is he, Christ, to everyone who believes. The word of faith that we preach is the righteousness of faith, in our hearts and in our mouths. Now we must confess that faith with our mouth, the Lord Jesus, and we shall believe in our hearts that our God has raised Jesus from the dead.

There is no way we can submit to the righteousness of God if we try to establish our own righteousness! Therefore, traditions of men, creed books, etc., are to be removed from our worship and praise given as the Holy Scriptures provide.

We are saved by this acceptance of grace of the Father, the acceptance of the Messiah, the Chosen One. Christ is grace! He is the unmerited favor.

Verse 10 of Romans chapter 10 says "for with the heart man believes unto righteousness and with the mouth confession is made unto salvation." There is no need to be ashamed to confess your Savior. So call upon Him!

Why should you confess your faults before men? Jesus put it this way in Mark 1:20-23:

> What comes from your heart is what makes you unclean. Out of your heart come evil thoughts, vulgar deeds, stealing, murder, unfaithfulness in marriage, greed, meanness, deceit, indecency, envy, insults, pride, and foolishness. All of these come from your heart, and they are what make you unfit to worship God.

At times in my life I was guilty of some of these 13 sins. It made me so ashamed and truly I was unfit to worship God. The only way I could cleanse my conscience of this shame was to confess it. The only way I could have hope in forgiveness was to confess it. The only way

I can grow as a Christian is to confess that I am not worthy to have received God's wonderful kindness (grace).

It is not what goes into a man that defiles him, it is what comes out of his heart!

Mark 7:15

> There is nothing from without a man that entering into him can defile him: but the things which come out of him, those are they that defile the man.

Jesus was so adamant about this issue that He said it again in verse 18 as well.

Simply put, confession is a must in the plan of salvation! "For with the heart man believes unto righteousness and with the mouth confession is made unto salvation."

BAPTISM

Jesus told John the Baptist to baptize Him to fulfill all righteousness. That act destroys the body of sin in New Testament Christians and brings us to the point where we can be resurrected incorruptible, just as Jesus was. It is an act of submission and conscience-cleansing and binds us with the Comforter that Jesus sent, disallowing sin to have dominion over us.

Surviving spiritually depends upon a change in your life. What can you do to make sure you have eternal salvation? Acts 2:38 says "change and be immersed in water, every one of you, in the name of Jesus Christ for the remission of sins, and you will receive the gift of the Comforter."

There are two blessings we get when we are immersed into Christ. We are told that remission or release of sin is the first gift, and then second, we receive the Comforter. To get these special blessings, we must hear the Word, believe it, change our attitude toward the Gospel, confess our sins, and be baptized in the name of Jesus Christ. Then we must be obedient to this calling.

Romans 6:3-4, 16-17

> Know you not that so many of us as were baptized (immersed) into Jesus Christ were baptized into His death? Therefore, we are buried with Him by baptism into death. That like as Christ was raised up from the dead by the glory of the Father, even so we also should walk in newness of life. For if we have been planted together in the likeness of His death, we shall be also in the likeness of His resurrection; knowing this, that our old man is crucified with Him, that the body of sin might be destroyed, that henceforth we should not serve sin. For He that is dead is freed from sin. Now if we be dead with Christ, we believe that we shall also live with Him. For in that He died, He died unto sin once, but in that He lives, He lives unto God. Likewise reckon you also yourselves to be dead indeed unto sin, but alive unto God through Jesus Christ our Lord. For ye are not under the law, but under grace! Sin shall have no dominion over you.

Mark 16:15-16

Jesus told us to go into the entire world and preach the Gospel to every person. He that believes and is immersed in water shall be saved, but he that believes not shall be damned. Then the Lord will work with us and confirm His words in our lives.

1 Peter 3:21

Yes! Salvation comes by grace and by water. "The like figure whereunto even baptism does also now save us (not the putting away of the filth of the flesh, but the answer of a good conscience toward God), by the resurrection of Jesus Christ who is gone into Heaven, and is on the right hand of God, angels and authorities and powers being made subject unto Him."

God wanted us to perform a ceremony in the act of immersion for the sole purpose of cleansing our conscience toward Him and in so doing prove to Him our conviction of His grace. The Bible teaches in several areas that if we believe we shall be saved. When we believe the entire sound doctrine of God's Word, we will obey all His desires and commands. Salvation by water and grace is a part of His divine plan, and we cannot separate it. Remember it is a "like figure" of the death, burial and resurrection of our personal Savior. All the Apostles taught this principle in their writings.

Need a Biblical example?

Acts 10:48

Some of those who have gone on before us were asked to be witnesses of all the things that Jesus did after God raised Him from the dead. No man could forbid water that one should be baptized. They were even commanded to be baptized in the name of Jesus.

WORKS

First of all, you must understand that your works do not save you, they only determine what reward to receive once your in Heaven.

Why are works so important in living the Christian life? Paul said it this way in Colossians 1:28-29: "We announce the message about

Jesus, and we use all our wisdom to warn and teach everyone, so that all of Christ's followers will grow in the spirit and become mature disciples of Christ."

Each man's work shall be made manifest as stated in 1 Corinthians 3:13-15:

> [13]For the day shall declare it, because it is revealed in fire! And the fire itself shall prove each man's work of what sort it is. [14]If any man's work shall abide which he built thereon, he shall receive a reward. [15]If any man's work shall be burned he shall suffer loss, but he himself shall be saved, yet so as through fire!

So! Our works done here on Earth will be tried in fire, whether good or bad. We will either receive a reward or suffer loss for those works. The salvation of our souls, however, depends upon judgments made by Christ Himself. So there must be degrees of reward in Heaven according to this scripture *(this is a personal opinion based on the scriptures we have just read).*

It states that we will receive a reward if our work makes it through the fire and suffer loss if it doesn't make it through the fire, but He goes on to say that our soul's salvation also is tried as through fire! The way I understand this is that even if I suffer loss (of reward) because my works don't withstand the trial through fire, I still can be saved. This is God's judgment and not mankind's.

There is no other foundation which a man can lay than that which is laid, which is Jesus Christ (1 Corinthians 3:11).

It is interesting to note that the Bible calls wisdom, righteousness, sanctification and redemption gifts in 1 Corinthians 1:30. We are commanded to not know anything among people, but Jesus crucified. So, everything we discuss among people not related to the death of

Jesus on the cross, and His sacrificing Himself for us, is irrelevant to salvation (1 Corinthians 2:2).

"For seeing that in the wisdom of God, the world through its wisdom did not even know God. But it was God's good pleasure through the foolishness of preaching to save them which believed in His plan." Preaching is a work. A very important one, according to 1 Corinthians 1:21, and yet is called foolishness. And this pleases our Creator because it is the most viable means of spreading the Word about His wonderful kindness.

In our works here on Earth we should not expect immediate praise from God because we are reminded "don't judge anything before the time the Lord comes back and who then will both bring to light the hidden things of darkness and make manifest the counsels of everyone's heart. Then and only then shall each man have his praise from God" (1 Corinthians 4:5).

Acts 17:30

It is important to note that God has set a day when He will judge the world with justice by the Man He has appointed. That man is Jesus Christ the Messiah! God the Father has given proof of this to all man by raising that same Man (Jesus) from the dead.

OBEDIENCE

Through obedience, we as true disciples (learners) apply the plan God gave us.

Even if we have all the faith that is discussed in the concept of grace, we must find a way to apply it to our everyday life. This is only accomplished by being obedient to that word which has been handed down to you. You now have substance, something to tie it all together to make hope work for you. In submission and obedience, faith becomes visible and it is the evidence God requires, even though we may still not fully understand the big picture.

However! We are also told in the Scriptures that faith without works is a dead faith. Jesus supplied the grace when He shed His blood. Without works of some sort, we still have not arrived at the place of service that God requires of us.

Here is the scripture to back up this statement (James 2:17-26):

> **Even so! Faith, if not shown through the actions of works, is dead, being alone. I show God my faith when I perform good works and perfect my submission to God as well as justify and befriend Him.**
>
> *Obedience through action would be a good biblical definition of works.*

Revelation 22:12

> Look, I am coming soon! My reward is with me, and I will give to each person according to what they have done. [*Epilogue: invitation and warning*]

My works never save me, but they do determine my reward once I get to Heaven.

Ephesians 6:8

> Because you know that the Lord will reward each one for whatever good they do, whether they are slave or free.

Hebrews 5:9

> And Christ, fulfilling perfection in His life here on Earth, became the author of eternal salvation unto all them that obey Him.

Hebrews 11:1-6

What we see physically here on Earth was not made by what is materialistic or visible. Without faith it is impossible to please God. We must believe that He exists and that He rewards us if we seek Him.

Hebrews 10:23

> Let us hold on to the hope we profess to have, because our Creator who made us the promises is the faithful one.

Romans 8:24-25

> For in unseen hope we are saved but hope that is seen is no hope at all. Who hopes for what he already has? But if we hope for what we do not yet have, we wait for it patiently.

1 Peter 1:17

> Since you pray through Jesus to a God who judges each man's work impartially, you are expected to live your lives as strangers here on Earth in reverent fear to that God.

1 Timothy 2:5

> For there is one God and one mediator between God and men: the man Christ Jesus who was equal to God, who gave Himself as a ransom for all men the testimony given in its proper time.

Acts 2:38

> Then Peter said unto them, repent and be immersed every one of you in the name of Jesus Christ for the remission of sins, and you shall receive the gift of the (Comforter) Holy Spirit.

Acts10:45

> And they of the circumcision (Jews) which believed were astonished, as many as came with Peter, because that on the Gentiles also was poured out the gift of the Holy Ghost.

John 14:16-17

> And Jesus will ask God the Father, and He will give you another counselor to be with you forever, who is the Spirit of Truth.

John 15:26

> When Jesus sends the counselor from the Father, the Spirit of Truth who goes out from the Father, will testify about who Jesus truly is.

51

John16:13

> But when the Spirit of Truth comes He will guide us into all truth however will not speak on His own but will speak only what He hears from God the Father and He will tell you what is yet to come and will bring glory to Jesus by taking from what is Jesus' and making it known to us. All that belongs to the Father is also Jesus'. That is why Jesus said the spirit will take from what is His and make it known to us.

Remember that love is where no fear abides, and there is no fear in perfect love. Where fear is, Satan will be there, and we do not want to dwell in fear for God is not there!

Romans 8:15, 26

> For we did not receive a spirit that makes us slaves again to fear: but we received the spirits of son-ship.

Now we must add to our faith, virtue temperance, patience, godliness, brotherly kindness and love.

We must come to an understanding as we grow as Christians that when we put on Christ in baptism, that we put on the character of Christ in His death, burial and resurrection from the dead. We stand for His cause and we are representing in our lives that the flesh is only a temporary dwelling place. Material places and things are not our goal. Just as Jesus' goal was not to remain in the tomb, to be sick, to be subjected to the grave and death, we too (our soul) in the spiritual realm will not be subjected to death, either. By putting on His personality as Christians we will win the victory over death and there will be no sting, no pain, no tears, no suffering and no night there in that heavenly dwelling place. The sting of rebuke and Eternal damnation will be to those of the synagogue (assembly) of Satan.

In Revelation 2, the letter to the angel of the Church at Pergamum, as Jesus had instructed John in a vision, this is what was written (verse 13): "I know where you live is where Satan has his throne. But you have kept true to my name." In verse 17: "To everyone who wins the victory, I will give him some of the hidden food. I will also give each one a white stone with a new name written on it. No one will know that name except the one who is given the stone."

Historians don't know exactly what the "white stone" refers to; however, some of the manna sent down from Heaven to the Israelites was placed in a jar and hidden in the sacred chest (Exodus 16). When the prophet Jeremiah hid the chest in a cave during the destruction of the temple by the Babylonians, the word was spread that only when God came to save His people would they be allowed to partake of the hidden food. Some believe that the "white stone" is a symbol of victory in Christ. Some believe it is the ticket which allows us as Christians to enter God's Rest on the Day of Judgment.

Either way, we have an inheritance into God's Kingdom if we don't give up our faith. Read what He said to tell the angels of the other six churches:

> To Ephesus: "I will let everyone who wins the victory eat from the life-giving tree in God's wonderful garden."

> To Smyrna: "Whoever wins the victory will not be hurt by the second death."

> To Thyatira: "I will give power over the nations to everyone who wins the victory and keeps on obeying me until the end. I will give them the power that my Father has given me. They will rule the nations with an iron rod and smash those nations to pieces like clay pots. I will also give them the morning star."

To Sardis: "Everyone who wins the victory will wear white clothes. Their names will not be erased from the Book of Life, and I will tell my Father and His angels that they are my followers."

To Philadelphia: "Everyone who wins the victory will be made into a pillar in the temple of my God, and they will stay there forever. I will write on each of them the name of my God and the name of His city. It is the New Jerusalem that my God will send down from Heaven. I will also write on them my own new name."

To Laodicea: "Everyone who wins the victory will sit with me on my throne; just as I won the victory and sat with my Father on His throne."

Very interesting! Did you notice that in every letter he also said this: "If you have ears, listen to what the Spirit says to the Churches."

All seven letters were meant to be heard by all seven churches. In Revelation 1:10, John said the Spirit took control of me and gave the message! This should show us how important the Holy Spirit is in guiding us today.

COMMUNION WITH CHRIST

Living the daily commitment in Christ is probably the hardest thing we can do. The following scriptures will help us understand why we have been commanded to remember daily, our one and only Savior, Jesus the Christ.

1 Corinthians10:16

The cup of blessing which we bless, isn't it the communion of the blood of Christ? The bread which we break, isn't it the communion of the body of Christ?

1 Corinthians 12:27

Now we as Christians are the body of Christ, and members in particular.

See Galatians 3:27 and Romans 7:4 concerning how we put on Christ and bear fruit.

Ephesians 4:12

Any communion we participate in is for the perfecting of the set apart souls called saints, for the work of the ministry, and for the edifying of the body of Christ which is called the Church.

2 Corinthians 6:14

Do not be unequally bonded together with unbelievers because what fellowship has righteousness with unrighteousness? And what communion has light with darkness?

2 Corinthians 13:14

The grace of the Lord Jesus Christ, and the love of God and the communion of the Holy Ghost, is with you all. Let it be!

Ephesians 2:13

> In Christ Jesus those who sometimes were lost are brought into the Body or church by the blood of Christ.

Hebrews 9:14

> How much more shall the blood of Christ, who through the eternal spirit offered himself without spot to God, cleanse your conscience from dead works to serve the living God?

In the memorial service we participate in called the Lord's Supper, God has established a way for us to give an account of the worthiness of our participation. Not that we can ever be "worthy" to receive the grace He freely gives, but we can be reconciled towards God in the acts of repentance, submission, obedience and humility. If we knowingly participate in a non-reconciled state of being, we are spiritually crucifying Christ all over again. This is plainly stated in the following scripture:

1 Corinthians 11:27

> Wherefore who ever will eat of this bread, and drink this cup of the Lord unworthily, will be guilty of the body and the blood of the Lord.

1 Corinthians 11:28

> But let a man examine himself first, and then eat of that bread and drink of that cup!

I take this to mean if I have something warring in my spirit against a brother, or my conscience will not allow me to participate in the memorial service justifiably, it is better to pass on the Lord's Supper. After my heart is right with God, then I should participate.

Luke 22:17

> And Jesus took the cup, and gave thanks to His Father, and said, take this, and divide it among yourselves.

Luke 22:20

After the supper, Jesus told the disciples that this cup is the New Testament in my blood, which is shed for you.

> How often must we participate in the memorial to Christ? I would say, consistently, steadfastly, just as the apostles did and as often as we do participate it should be as the examples were given.

The scriptures make clear that the disciples were very consistent not only in the memorial service to the Lord but in study, fellowship, and prayer according to Acts 2:42.

> And they continued steadfastly in the apostles' doctrine and fellowship, and in breaking of bread, and in prayers.

Matthew 26:26

> And as they were eating, Jesus took bread, and blessed it, and broke it, and gave it to the disciples and said, take, eat, this is my body.

This same statement is also found in Mark 14.

John 6:41

The Jews then murmured at Him because He said,
"I am the bread which came down from Heaven."

John 6:48

Jesus said repeatedly, "I am that bread of life"! Bread is substance,
evidence, a manifestation and principles and truth. Eat the living
bread and live.

John 6:50

This is the bread which cometh down from Heaven,
that a man may eat thereof, and not die.

John 6:51

I am the living bread, which came down from
Heaven and if any man eats of this bread, he will
live forever, and the bread I will give is my flesh, and
I will give for the life of the world.

John 6:58

This is the bread which came down from Heaven,
not like the manna your fathers ate and now are
dead. He that eats of this bread will live forever.

John 6:33

For the bread of God is Jesus which cometh down
from Heaven and gives life unto the world.

John 6:35

> And Jesus said unto them, I am the bread of life. He
> that cometh to me will never hunger, and he that
> believes on me will never thirst.

The Lord's Supper is remembering Jesus' life, death, burial, and
resurrection from the dead. This is a memorial ceremony and has
nothing to do with cannibalism as some would have you to believe.

Luke 22:19

> And He took bread, gave thanks, broke it and gave
> unto them saying, this is my body, which is given for
> you, so do it in remembrance of me.

The fruit of the vine! The symbol of Christ Blood.

Hebrews 9:22

The law requires that nearly everything be cleansed with blood, and
without the shedding of blood there is no forgiveness.

> He did not enter the most holy place by means of the
> blood of bulls and goats and calves; having obtained
> eternal redemption.

> And in **Hebrews 9:11-14**: How much more, then,
> will the blood of Christ, who through the eternal
> Spirit offered Himself unblemished to God, cleanse
> our consciences from acts that lead to death, so that
> we may serve the living God!

Mark 14:23

> And He took the cup, and when He had given thanks, He gave it to them, and they all drank of it.

Mark 26:27

> And He took the cup, and gave thanks, and gave it to them, saying, drink ye all of it.

I have referred to all the above scriptures to show the consistency and importance participation in the Lord's Supper was for the first disciples, and for Christians today.

CHAPTER 5

SAVING BY BOTH FEAR AND LOVE FROM THE SECOND DEATH

There is an attitude portrayed by Christians of old that no matter what it took to save a soul from hellfire, they would do it. It is rare to hear a lesson on hellfire and brimstone as were given not too many years ago. It is very important to let you know that Hell is real, and Satan is real, and his demons are active today just like they were from the first day he fell from grace.

The value is that accepting this lesson should create in us a sense of urgency to save ourselves from eternal damnation and love our brothers enough to save them as well. We should feel the same way about leading people to Christ, and no matter what it takes to convert a soul from the error of their ways, it is our responsibility to do so. We should consider that conversion of a soul leads to the "hiding of a multitude of sin" (James 5:19-20).

This is what the Scriptures means when the writers talk about admonishing and exhorting. They did it in love just as I try to do, but to the carnal-minded person, those who even proclaim to be atheist and say there is no God, it takes a boldness we sometimes don't know how to express. That is why I admire the Apostle Paul so much. I know why God chose Paul, and that only a select number of men could proclaim what Jesus needed to proclaim through men at that time. He was set apart! (Ephesians 4:12)

Jesus was dealing with people who still were taught and convinced that the Mosaic Law had to be abided by, and yet Jesus had just eliminated that dispensation by dying for those people.

Yes! That period of law that God Himself implemented had now passed, just as the patriarchal law had been superseded by the Law of Moses (the Ten Commandments). Now the Law of Grace (God's simple wonderful kindness) had superseded the law which could never be lived up to by God's own chosen race.

Now there is a law (the Law of Grace) that we as Christians do not have to have our sins brought up every year and remembered. Our sin, through the blood of Christ, is totally forgotten and remembered no more. The only responsibility God expects from His children is to love Him, keep His commandments and participate in reconciling others back to him . He also expects us to look for mercy in the Judgment Day and expect it as has been promised. God will keep His promises. So, what is this all about? Read on!

Jude 21-23

> Christians! You must stay in the love of God, looking for the mercy of our Lord Jesus Christ unto eternal life. And on some have compassion, making a difference through love; and others save them with fear if necessary, pulling them out of the fire and hating even the garment spotted by the flesh.

Revelation 20:14

> And death and hell were cast into the Lake of Fire. This is the second death.

Revelation 20:10

And Satan the great deceiver who hindered the lost was cast into the Lake of Fire and brimstone, where also the beast and the false prophet are, and he shall be tormented day and night for ever and ever.

Revelation 21:6-8

And Jesus said unto me, it is done. I am alpha and omega, the beginning and the end. I will give unto him that is athirst of the fountain of the water of life freely. He that overcomes shall inherit all things and I will be his God, and he shall be my son. But the fearful, and unbelieving, and the abominable, and murderers, and whoremongers, and sorcerers, and idolaters, and all liars, shall have their part in the lake which burns with fire and brimstone, which is the second death.

Revelation 2:10-11

Fear none of those things which you shall suffer; behold, Satan will cast some of you into prison, that ye may be tried, and ye will have tribulation ten days, but be thou faithful unto death, and I will give thee a crown of life. He that hath an ear let him hear what the spirit says unto the churches, he that overcomes shall *not* be hurt of the second death.

Jude 5

Verse 7: God does save and destroy!

Those who are destroyed will suffer the vengeance of eternal fire!

> Verses 11-13: Those who are destroyed will suffer in the blackness of darkness forever.

Once again!

We are taught to both save by love and by fear. Just remember this fear (reverence for Almighty God) is also fear of spending eternity in the Lake of Fire away from the presence of God. We are not to fear man or what he can do to us physically, but to reverence the One who can send our soul to hell.

Jude vs. 21-23

The phrase "pulling them out of the fire; hating even the garment spotted by the flesh" is very powerful in that this is a command to reach out to the lost. We are expected to snatch those lost souls away from Satan. If we don't pull them out of the fire and help them see the light and we have ability to do so, we are letting Satan control our lives. It is important that we abhor the evil in our world. Entertainment alone distracts us from hating evil. It makes it lucrative and enjoyable to participate in while we are carnally minded. God said that there would be pleasure in sin! This is the "garment spotted by the flesh" that is the lust in our world!

We must just make up our minds that we will not let the pleasure of sin control us, and actively hate sin in our world. For a person who is controlled by lust and materialism, love may not be the only way to pull them away! We must be strong enough in our conviction to say it the way it is. Hell is real and there will be weeping and gnashing of teeth and the worm will never die. It will be miserable in Hell! More so, just being denied the presence of Almighty God and His love for eternity will be unmentionable sadness and misery.

If we truly love those who have been pulled into the fire of lust, we must let them know the Scriptures concerning reprobates. To be classified as a reprobate is sad! Those who no longer have approval by God are those of reprobate concerning the faith, corrupt minds with no part in eternal salvation.

Romans 1:21-32

[21]Because that, when they knew God, they glorified Him not as God, neither were thankful; but became vain in their imaginations, and their foolish heart was darkened. [22] Professing themselves to be wise, they became fools, [23]and changed the glory of the uncorruptible God into an image made like to corruptible man, and to birds, and four-footed beasts, and creeping things. *[24]Wherefore God also gave them up to uncleanness through the lusts of their own hearts, to dishonor their own bodies between themselves*: [25]Who changed the truth of God into a lie and worshipped and served the creature more than the Creator, who is blessed forever. Amen. [26]For this cause *God gave them up unto vile affections*: for even their women did change the natural use into that which is against nature: [27]And likewise also the men, leaving the natural use of the woman, burned in their lust one toward another; men with men working that which is unseemly, and *receiving in themselves that recompense of their error which was meet.* [28]And even as *they did not like to retain God in their knowledge, God gave them over to a reprobate mind,* to do those things which are not convenient; [29]being filled with all unrighteousness, fornication, wickedness, covetousness, maliciousness; full of envy, murder,

> debate, deceit, malignity; whisperers, [30]backbiters, haters of God, despiteful, proud, boasters, inventors of evil things, disobedient to parents, [31]without understanding, covenant breakers, without natural affection, implacable, unmerciful: [32]Who knowing the judgment of God, that they which commit such things are worthy of death, not only do the same, but have pleasure in them that do them.

If we teach a person who is in the "spirit of error" to become the "spirit of truth" by fear, we must also show them that love perfects the fear as we grow in Christ.

1 John 4:15-21

> Those who confess that Jesus is the Son of God, God dwells in him, and he in God. And we have known and believed the love that God has for us. God is love; and he that dwells in love dwells in God and God in him. Herein is our love made perfect, that we may have boldness in the Day of Judgment; because as He is so are we in this world. There is no fear in love; but perfect love casts out fear; because fear hath torment. He that fears is not made perfect in love. We love Him, because He first loved us. If a man says I love God, and hates his brother, he is a liar; for he that loves not his brother whom he has seen, how can he love God; whom he has not seen? And the commandment we have from Him is that he who loves God loves his brother also.

The spirits of truth and error! Simply put they are 1) "The spirits of believers that Jesus is the Son of God," and 2) "spirits of antichrist" (1 John 4:3-6).

1 John 4:5

> They are of the world (all of the antichrist, verse 3); so, all they speak of is the world and the world hears them.

> We (1 John 4:6) are of God: he that knows God hears us; he that is not of God doesn't hear us. Hereby we know the spirit of truth and the spirit of error.

Now is the last time! The antichrists are many and are those who deny Jesus and His claim to be the only begotten Son of God.

1 John 2:18-25

> Little children, it is the last time: and as ye have heard that antichrist will come, even now are there many antichrists: whereby we know that it is the last time.

> ²²Who is a liar? but he that denies that Jesus is the Christ? He is antichrist that denies the Father and the Son.

Jesus came to Earth for one reason: to destroy the works of the Devil!

1 John 3:7-8

> Little children let no man deceive you: he that doeth righteousness is righteous, even as he is righteous. He that commits sin is of the devil; for the devil sins from the beginning. For this purpose, the Son of God was manifested, that He might destroy the works of the devil.

Steve C. Varner

1 John 1:2-4

> (for the life was manifested, and we have seen it, and
> bear witness, and show unto you that eternal life,
> which was with the Father, and was manifested unto
> us;) that which we have seen and heard declare we
> unto you, that ye also may have fellowship with us;
> and truly our fellowship is with the Father, and with
> His Son Jesus Christ. And these things we write to
> you, that your joy may be full.

1 Peter 3:15-22

> [15]This is your answer of the reason of the hope
> within you!

> [21]Baptism does save us by cleansing our conscience
> toward God! By the resurrection of Jesus Christ!

1 Peter 4:16-17

Don't be ashamed to confess Christ!

Don't deny obedience in the Word and face judgment without the
spirit of truth!

Come out of the spirit of error into the spirit of truth!

You have heard the Word. Do you believe it?

Does this teaching through love and/or fear lead you to change?

Do you have enough courage to confess your faith before men today?

Are you willing to be immersed into Christ for the remission of your sin and receive the gift of the Comforter? (Galatians 3:27)

Are you prepared to sacrifice your life to obedience to God's will?

Are you dedicated enough to show your faith by your works, knowing they will be tried in fire in the Judgment Day?

Are you willing to add to your faith, temperance, godliness, patience, brotherly kindness and love?

If it takes love, God has said He will never forsake thee or leave thee! God has prepared a mansion just for you; there will be no more sorrow, no tears, and no darkness. His promises are exceeding above and beyond all we can imagine.

If it takes fear, isn't it enough to know that there will be weeping and gnashing of teeth, that the worm will never die, that the Abyss is the blackest of darkness, that whatever suffering there is in the Lake of Fire and brimstone that no water is available to quench the pain and you don't want to go there? Absence of the presence of God is unthinkable to me!

What hinders you? Find the water! Ask a Christian to baptize you in the name of the Father, the Son and the Holy Spirit. Begin your journey and take someone you love with you.

CHAPTER 6

THINGS I LEARNED WHILE READING THE BIBLE

Satan has his very own synagogue (assembly); all the evil handed down originally came from him (Revelation 2:9).

Satan has one goal in mind. He seeks to destroy us! He seeks to create an environment of terror if the world exists (1 Peter 5:8).

There are two types of death mentioned in the Bible:

- The first death is the death of the physical body which all must bear.
- The second death is the everlasting spiritual death, and as a child of God I don't have to bear that one (Revelation 2:11).

If I believe in Christ, no matter how much I am ridiculed or persecuted, I will never be put to shame (1 Peter 2:6).

People can be saved by both fear and love. However, it is not the fear of man or Satan that causes us to be saved. So the extremist mentality of doing what they do violently for their god is total hogwash. God teaches us to abhor all evil deeds (Jude 22).

God not only saves men, but He destroys them as well. "God is a jealous God." He would not have any one of us perish, but He gives us the opportunity to love Him back.

Exodus 34:14

> For thou shalt worship no other god: for the Lord, whose name is Jealous, is a jealous God.

Deuteronomy 4:24

> For the Lord thy God is a consuming fire, even a jealous God.

> He is the most kind of all beings as He has given us opportunity to share in His Glory. If we do not accept that offer, we will share in eternal damnation and terror of His everlasting absence.

Jude 5

It is wrong to bid anyone Godspeed unless he is a believer in Christ. If we do, we participate in their evil deeds. If we know it is wrong and do it anyway, it then becomes sin (2 John:10-11).

The antichrist is not a single person but is many. The Bible plainly speaks of many antichrists, no matter what you have heard people say about them or him! Check out the words John wrote about the antichrist in 2 John 7, and 1 John 2:18-22.

God only hears us if we ask according to His will. Ask something of God just because you desire it for selfish reasons and He probably will not even hear it. If you ask it to be so if it is His will I am sure He will hear it and answer according to whether it is beneficial to you at the time. God said He would never forsake you or leave you.

You must be the one to have faith that He will do what He said He would do (1 John 5:14).

There are only two types of spirits in the world: truth and error. Compare them to right and wrong. Good and bad. Kind and evil. Straight and narrow. Heaven and hell. Ignorance and understanding, darkness and light, pleasure and pain. It all makes sense when we look at the big picture (1 John 4:6).

Christ came into the world to destroy the works of the devil. Before Christ came in the form of man, Satan had already set up his evil plan of deception and corruption. He had his victory in death, which was physical death. When Christ died, was buried and then rose from the dead, He took that victory away from Satan. Satan no longer has any victory! He is doomed (1 John 3:8).

Christians can be led away from salvation by the error of the wicked and fall from grace and their own steadfastness. This eliminates the doctrine of "once saved, always saved."

2 Peter 3:17

> Ye therefore, beloved, seeing ye know these things before, beware lest ye also, being led away with the error of the wicked, fall from your own steadfastness.

Hebrews 6:4-6

> For it is impossible for those who were once enlightened, and have tasted of the heavenly gift, and were made partakers of the Holy Ghost, and have tasted the good Word of God, and the powers of the world to come, if they shall fall away, to renew them again unto repentance; seeing they crucify to themselves the Son of God afresh, and put Him to an open shame.

2 Peter 3:17

> The gift of grace or wonderful kindness can be taken away from us simply by our disobedience to God's will even if we once have experienced it.

1 John 2:1

Anytime we sin we have an advocate who will go before Almighty God on our behalf if we ask Him. God wants us to communicate through the mediator He gave us, who is Jesus. Everything we ask for should be asked in the name of Jesus Christ. Continuing in sin, however, just because we know we have the Advocate, is not acceptable to God. Remember that there is a difference between knowing to do right and sinning anyway and sinning out of our ignorance.

The moon and stars and Earth with all the works people do will melt some day with fervent heat. Right now, it all is just being kept in store reserved unto fire. The first time the Earth was destroyed by water and only a few were saved.

Genesis 9:11-13

> I will establish my covenant with you, neither shall all flesh be cut off any more by the waters of a flood; neither shall there anymore be a flood to destroy the Earth.

> [12] And God said, this is the token of the covenant which I make between me and you and every living creature that is with you, for perpetual generations:[13] I do set my bow in the cloud, and it shall be for a token of a covenant between me and the Earth.

The rainbow was not created for nor does it have anything to do with gay pride.

The next time God destroys the Earth it will be by fire, and even the firmaments and planets will melt.

2 Peter 3:7-11

> [7] But the heavens and the Earth, which are now, by the same word are kept in store, reserved unto fire against the Day of Judgment and perdition of ungodly men.

The Creator allows us to suffer a while to make us perfect, establish, strengthen and settle us, and to bring Him glory (1 Peter 4:14-16 and 5:10; Philippians 12:7-30)

1 Peter 3:17

> It is better for us to suffer for doing well than it is for us to suffer for doing evil.

Some people create their own destruction because they are unlearned and wrestle with the hard things to understand in the Bible. There are a lot of things I have not addressed in the Bible because I have not studied it in detail enough to comment on it. It is important that I don't struggle with some of the hard things in the Bible, just as this scripture says. If I study like I am instructed to do, and understand the simple plan of salvation, I will not create destruction for myself (2 Peter 3:16).

The act of baptism does save us through grace. Belief is one of the prerequisites to baptism. We are buried in the likeness of His death and in the likeness of His resurrection and our bodies of sin are destroyed by the act of cleaning our conscience (1 Peter 3:21; Galatians 3:27; Romans 6:3-14; Romans 4:15).

Jesus Christ never sinned, however He was tempted, just as we are (1 Peter 2:21; Hebrews 4:15-16).

It is a command for us never to swear or we will fall into condemnation. I take it to mean we are not to use God's name in vain. I think this is the same as blaspheming the Holy Spirit (James 5:12).

If we convert a sinner from the error of his ways, we save a soul from death and hide a multitude of sins (James 5:20).

If I know to do well and don't do it, to me it is sin (James 4:17).

If you will resist the devil he will run away from you. So, remember if you choose to resist the terrorism and violence, its impact on your life vanishes because the fear will not be there once you acquire a working relationship with your Creator (James 4:7).

Faith without works is dead (James 2:24-26).

The devils believe in Jesus and even tremble at His name (James 2:19).

God does not tempt us (James 1:13).

God is a consuming fire (Hebrews 12:29).

We unknowingly entertain angels (Hebrews 13:2).

There will come a day when God will not only shake the Earth, but He will also shake Heaven (Hebrews 12:26).

There will never be another offering for our sins. Christ blood and body was enough for God (Hebrews 10:16-18).

The first covenant God made with man had faults and God decided to change His laws. He changed the patriarchal law, which was speaking through the fathers, and then He changed the Mosaic Law, which was the Ten Commandments. The final law is the Law of Grace which we continue to live under. This is the Christian dispensation (Hebrews 8:7 through 10:39).

The Word of God can never be bound (2 Timothy 2:9).

The Bible teaches that using a little wine helps our infirmities. It also teaches that drunkards will not inherit the Kingdom of God. Even though it is pure, it also teaches that if it causes a brother to be made weak or stumble, it is not a good thing (1 Timothy 5:23; 1 Corinthians 6:9-12; Romans 14:21).

The Apostles taught that a woman should learn in silence. They went so far as to tell them to say it was a shame for them to speak in the Church (1 Timothy 2:11; 1 Corinthians 14:34-35).

There is one God and one mediator between God and man (1 Timothy 2:5).

The Lord Jesus will take vengeance in flaming fire on all of those who have troubled us as Christians and they will be punished with everlasting destruction from the presence of the Lord. This is a righteous thing with God (2 Thessalonians 1:6-9).

When Jesus returns the next time all the Christians who have died will rise incorruptible and then those of us Christians who are alive at that time will be caught up together with them in the clouds to meet the Lord in the air. Then we shall be with Him forever. We all will be changed from a corruptible being into an incorruptible, immortal being just as fast as a blink of the eye (1 Thessalonians 4:16-17; 1 Corinthians 15:52-54).

If we serve the Lord Jesus Christ, we will receive a reward of the inheritance in the Kingdom of Almighty God. We will share in His glory there (Colossians 3:24-25).

In Jesus Christ dwells the fullness of the Godhead Bodily. He is the head of all principality and power. When we are baptized (immersed) we are raised with Christ through the faith of the operation of God, who raised Jesus from the dead. So being dead in our sins Jesus quickens us together with Him and forgives us all our trespasses. God the Father, Christ, the (Holy Spirit dwelling in men and woman) all share in the Godhead if we are believers.

I am the temple of God and if I defile my body He will destroy me. The Godhead is also not like precious material things or things made by men's hands (Colossians 2:8-15; Colossians 1:13-20; 1 Corinthians 11:3; 1 John 4:12-16; 1 Corinthians 3:17; Acts 17:29). We are told in the Scriptures that those who abuse Gods natural sexual plan will be given over to a reprobate mind (one not acceptable to Almighty God).

Titus 1:16

> They profess that they know God; but in works they
> deny Him, being abominable, and disobedient, and
> unto every good work reprobate.

Romans 1:28

> And even as they did not like to retain God in their
> knowledge, God gave them over to a reprobate
> mind, to do those things which are not convenient.

Homosexuals are worthy of death, just like multiple classifications of people who also are worthy of death. This chapter is worth reading for sure (Romans 1:18-32).

I can do all things through Christ which strengthens me (Philippians 4:13).

Jesus was in the form of God and didn't think it was robbery for Him to be equal with God (Philippians 2:6).

I can be angry as a Christian, however not let the sun go down before I overcome my anger and sin not (Ephesians 4:26-27).

I am instructed to abhor that which is evil (Romans 12:9-21).

We live under a law of grace—exceeding wonderful kindness (Ephesians 3).

Satan works in the children of disobedience and he is the prince of the power of the air. At one time we all were associated with him and were the children of wrath by nature (Ephesians 2:1-3).

I am not under the old law because I am led by the spirit. The letter (Mosaic Law) kills and the spirit gives us life. The law is the strength of sin and sin is the sting of death (Galatians 5:18; 2 Corinthians 3:6; 1 Corinthians 15:56).

Observing holidays is a questionable thing for us as Christians to get involved in, and it is possibly a dangerous thing to do. This is a hard thing for me to understand. I am not going to let it lead me to destruction, as 2 Peter 3:16 said it will do if I let it. I must accept it because Paul himself told the disciples that he was somewhat against them for these observances. That is enough for me to accept it. I have now learned not to put great emphasis on any holiday (Galatians 4:9-11).

I think I have possibly figured out what the Apostle Paul's thorn in the flesh was! It could have been an artifact in his physical appearance. However, I personally think it was the fact that he was rude, and very, very boastful in his speeches before the public and before the brethren, even to the point of saying, "lest he should be exalted above measure through the revelations he received that there was given to him a messenger of Satan to buffet him." He calls this his thorn in the flesh. He also goes on to say, "he used sharpness according to the power which the Lord gave him to edification and not to destruction." Why would God choose such a personality to do the job Paul did? Perhaps it was simply that Paul was not afraid to step on Satan's toes and face the punishments that followed (2 Corinthians 11:10; 2 Corinthians 12:7-11).

We are told to not be unequally yoked together with unbelievers; however, we are told that if an unbelieving spouse chooses to stay with us, we should not depart from them (2 Corinthians 6:14-18; 1 Corinthians 7).

Satan has the power to hide the Gospel from those who do not believe and are lost. Therefore, I titled my book *Satan: Still under Christ Kingdom's Scrutiny* because it is our responsibility to help those who are blinded, lost, or do not believe (2 Corinthians 4:3-4).

Physical death, as we know it now, will be the last enemy that shall be destroyed (1 Corinthians 15:26).

Those who have the gift of multiple languages (speaking in tongues) are only to speak during worship services if they have an interpreter. If not, they are to keep silence in the church. The use of multiple languages was intended for those who don't believe the Gospel. I have an interpreter in my job who speaks Russian, Kazak and English very well. She has a gift of tongues for sure, but she studied to learn those languages. I am sure some apostles were given the gift through the Holy Spirit. The understanding of tongues is hard for people who never have to have interpreters in their everyday life. This is not such an awe-inspiring thing for me. If I didn't have her help, it sure would sound like a clanging cymbal with no meaning (1 Corinthians 14:27-28; see also verse 22).

No man can say that Jesus is the Lord unless he is directed by the Holy Spirit to do so (1 Corinthians 12:3).

Even though it was by nature a shame for a man to have long hair, the Apostle told us that there was no custom within the church of Christ or by the apostles of Christ. So, no commands or condemnations were made if a man was contentious about his hair (1 Corinthians 11:14-16).

To me, as a Christian, all things are lawful; however, all things are not expedient, and they don't always edify other people. If I wound one's weak conscience by taking advantage of my liberty as a Christian and it becomes a stumbling block to them, I also commit sin. I should have enough self-control to the point where I am not brought under the power of anything. I am free from the law of sin and death (the Law of Moses) and there is no condemnation to me (1 Corinthians 10:23; 1 Corinthians 8:8-13; 1 Corinthians 6:12; Romans 8:1-2 and verse 10; Romans 6:14). I live under the Law of Grace!

If I am bound to a wife I should not seek to be loosed from her. Likewise, if I am not married I should not seek one either, unless I cannot contain myself sexually (1 Corinthians 7:27-40; 1 Corinthians 7:9).

It is wrong for me to withhold sex from my wife unless we agree on it for a period. Likewise, it is as wrong for her to withhold herself from me (1 Corinthians 7).

All the works I do while here on Earth will be tried by fire (1 Corinthians 3:13).

God has saved us and called us with a holy calling, not according to our works, but according to His own purpose and grace which was given to us in Christ before time began (2 Timothy 1:8-13). Our works only determine the degree of reward we receive.

Christ does save us by His grace and purpose, and not by our own works! But we are told that our faith without works is dead (James 2:24-26).

God does not save us according to the degree of our works, however; our faith is still dead without works. Read the 13th verse of 2 Timothy 1:8-13. Paul tells them to "Hold fast the pattern of sound words which you have heard from me, in faith and love which are in Christ Jesus." The message here is that we cannot let our emotions, feelings, and false scriptural values of those who claim to believe cause us to err from truth—the divinely inspired Word of God.

The Bible has a pattern to it, and to deviate from it in its entirety is to err from the truth. Remember that there are only two paths in life to follow: the path of truth or the path of error. There are no middle or outside pathways. Jesus is the Way, the truth, and the life, and no one will enter the Kingdom of Heaven without going through Him. Straight is the path that leads to righteousness, and few there be that find it. Broad is the path that leads to destruction, and many there be who will follow it.

Preaching is both foolishness and the power of God (1 Corinthians 1:17-25).

I must avoid anyone who causes strife concerning the doctrine of Christ (Romans 16:17).

When I allow wrong things to happen in my life, I can still be happy. I may be self-condemning (Romans 14:22).

Even though I am hurt, vengeance is not mine (Romans 12:17-21).

God is a God of second chances (Romans 11:23).

I am to hope for the things I cannot see with the naked eye (Romans 8:24-25).

I am only a friend to Jesus if I obey His commandments (John 15:10-27).

I have a Comforter who will remind me of all the promises I inherit as a Christian (John 14:26).

I have a place prepared for me in Heaven now if I am obedient to God in His great plan (John 14:1-3).

Jesus did believe in and had the power to answer deathbed confessions, even if it deviated from His written and divinely inspired plan of salvation as given in the New Testament. The thief on the cross was on his deathbed. Just by the act of confession that "truly this was the Son of God" to the other thief, Jesus granted him entry into paradise the same day.

The thief did not have to change much about his life, except for the change in his heart. He did repent on his deathbed, and he did confess; surely, he believed after what he saw happening to Jesus. We can assume that he had heard about Jesus claiming to be the Son of Almighty God by his statement, however Jesus did not require that he be baptized (immersed in water for the remission of sins), nor that he live a long obedient life. His life was almost over. I know he did not have to perform very many works as we are commanded, but he did exhibit faith because he asked Jesus to remember him when he entered His Kingdom!

So, the thief may have shown his faith by the single work of confession before all those who witnessed the crucifixion that day. One thing I am sure of is that our Lord and Savior has the power and the authority to make any changes if He desires to do so. It would be wrong for me to condemn anyone for deathbed repentance. As for us who are healthy, we are commanded to follow the plan He has given (Luke 23:39-43).

The Lord looks from Heaven and He sees all His creation. In His dwelling place He can look on all the inhabitants of the Earth and He fashions their hearts individually, He considers all of their works (Psalm 33:13-15).

CHAPTER 7

THE LEGEND OF EPIPHANY FROST
(THE CONTROVERSY OF OBSERVING DAYS)

Romans 14

> Those flood waters were like baptism that now saves you, but baptism is more than just washing your body. It means turning to God with a clear conscience, because Jesus Christ was raised from death. Christ is now in Heaven where He sits at the right side of God. All angels, authorities and powers are under His control.

1 Peter 3:21-22

Peter is referring to the flood that Noah and his family were saved from. He likens that immersion of the world to the baptism that now saves us.

There are special days observed, such as the Epiphany (the day Jesus was baptized), in some parts of the world that the early church was advised not to participate in. While remembering that Jesus Christ was in fact baptized to fulfill God's will is an event we need to keep in our minds, the Apostles themselves warned followers of Christ that observing special days could be dangerous (Galatians 4:9-11).

> ⁹But now, after that ye have known God, or rather
> are known of God, how turn ye again to the weak
> and beggarly elements, whereunto ye desire again
> to be in bondage? ¹⁰Ye observe days, and months,
> and times, and years. ¹¹I am afraid of you, lest I have
> bestowed upon you labor in vain.

Legend has it in certain circles that if you drink or wash in water sometime around January 6th you will be cleansed, and the following year will be a good one. There is also speculation that no bacterium grows in water collected on this day. Very interesting submissions indeed, but what does the Scripture say about this kind of observation?

I must accept the fact that Paul himself told the brothers in Galatia that he was somewhat against them for these types of observances. That is enough for me, if he said it. I have now learned not to put great emphasis on any holiday. You can read it!

It is a good time to remember what Peter said about Paul (2 Peter 3:14-18—don't twist the Scriptures, and don't lose balance):

> Don't forget that the Lord is patient because He
> wants people to be saved. This is also what our dear
> friend Paul said when he wrote you with the wisdom
> that God had given him. Paul talks about these same
> things in all his letters, but part of what he says is
> hard to understand. Some ignorant and unsteady
> people even destroy themselves by twisting what he
> said. They do the same thing with other scriptures
> too. My dear friends, you have been warned ahead
> of time! So, don't let the errors of evil people lead
> you down the wrong path and make you lose your
> balance.

Paul had just passed through Rome and taught the brethren there these words concerning the issue of criticizing others: "Some of the Lord's followers think one day is more important than another. Others think all days are the same. But each of you should make up your own mind. Any followers who count one day more important than another day do it to honor their Lord. And any followers who eat meat give thanks to God, just like the ones who don't eat meat."

If I just stopped here without trying to conclude what Paul's wisdom was in these two statements, I too could easily twist the context and wind up off-balance. But by reading on to the end of chapter 14 of Romans, I find that Paul concludes with this statement, in verse 22:

"What you believe about these things should be kept between you and God." You are fortunate if your actions don't make you have doubts. But if you do have doubts about what you eat, you are going against your own beliefs. And you know that is wrong, because anything you do against your beliefs is sin.

He goes on in the 15th chapter to describe how we are to be patient with the followers whose faith may not be as strong as ours. So, whether it is a question of eating certain things, drinking, observing certain holidays, or whatever may be of concern to a follower of the Lord, it is our place to "have patience, try to please them and not upset their faith." I should help the new convert or non-believer understand that the importance is on God's plan for salvation and let the trivial fall into place. It will take you time to understand Paul's wisdom, but be assured God did give it to him. Titus 1:10-14 may help in understanding His mentality.

We have learned that to have hope in the glory of Christ, He must be inside of us. So that means I better get Him inside of me if I am going to have any hope of glory after this life is over. There are specific directions given in Galatians 3:27 that "for as many of us that have been baptized into Christ have put on Christ." This means we have put on the character which He portrayed when He died on the cross, was buried, and raised again and ascended into Heaven.

The act of baptism is the tie that binds the human conscious and the spiritual Comforter. This tie is accomplished through faith and grace. Belief is one of the prerequisites to baptism. Hearing, confession, repentance, obedience, prayer, communion, fellowship, temperance, patience, kindness, and brotherly love are also requirements we must add to our faith. We are buried in the likeness of His death and in the likeness of His resurrection and our bodies of sin are destroyed by the act of cleaning our conscience (1 Peter 3:21; Galatians 3:27; Romans 6:3-14; Romans 4:15).

The reason it is so important to help others understand that this command is necessary to get to Heaven is stated in the following scripture: "If we convert a sinner from the error of his way we save a soul from death and hide a multitude of sins" (James 5:20).

Not believing in the power of baptism is the same as not believing in Christ. It would be the same as denying that Jesus implemented sanctification by His example of His own baptism and fulfillment of righteousness. That is exactly what He did. He implemented a way for us to have sin remitted or taken away, and at the same time implemented a way for the Holy Spirit of Promise (our guarantee) to enter the saved person. Jesus was the one who initiated the Law of Grace through His blood sacrifice.

This is conversion of a sinner from the error of his way. God has said when baptism is performed in the name of the Father, the Son, and the Holy Spirit, a multitude of sins are hidden, and this is the point at which we receive remission of our sins and receive the gift of the Comforter. Do you realize how important that is to God? Do you realize how important that is to you, the one doing the baptizing, and how important it is to the one who has just been baptized? It was so important to Jesus that He set an example, even though He could not possibly have been led from the error of His way because He had no error. He couldn't have a multitude of sins hidden, because He had no sin! This is truly why the day Jesus was baptized is so important—not regarding any day, just the reason He did so!

So why did He ask John to baptize Him? It was the ultimate act of the fulfillment of righteousness. He already was free from error, and He already was free from sin, He just wanted us to see the importance of completing righteousness in our lives through the act. It is an act of submission to His will. If we have not been baptized into Christ we have not completed righteousness in our life, because sin has not been hidden, nor error eliminated (remission of our sin) in us and the Holy Spirit cannot dwell in us and guide us. We have not cleansed our conscience toward God (1 Peter 3:21).

The like figure whereunto even baptism doth also now save us (not the putting away of the filth of the flesh, but the answer (or Pledge) of a good conscience toward God), by the resurrection of Jesus Christ: "If I know to do well and don't do it, to me it is sin" (James 4:17).

"If you will resist the devil he will run away from you. Anyone who tells you can be saved by man-made creeds is of the devil" (James 4:7).

There will never be another offering for our sins. Christ blood and body sacrifices were enough for God, while the blood of bulls and goats were not. When Jesus asked to be baptized He was confirming His own death, burial, and resurrection which He knew he had to experience soon. He proclaimed his future demise in Matthew 16:21. Jesus knew he would be laying down his life and knew he would be quickened in the Spirit and take his life back again. (John 10:11-18)

It is very interesting that in comparing ancient translations of the Aramaic Syriac Peshitta (the language Jesus spoke) versions of the Bible it says in Matthew 27:46 says;

[46] About three in the afternoon Jesus cried out in a loud voice, *"Eli, Eli, lema sabachthani?"* (which means "My God, my God, why have you forsaken me?") or ("for this was I spared or kept"). (some translations say; "Why have you spared me"?). Was Jesus' statement here a cry of desperation or a final declaration of his messiahship from Psalm 22:1? Because of his knowing the suffering to come, I personally believe it was in fact a statement confirming he completed his role, "it is finished".

"It is finished" is the translation of the Greek term "tetelestai."

It is the perfect indicative mood of the Greek verb "teleō," which means "to bring to an end" or "to complete.". see John 19:30

"For I have come down from heaven, not to do My own will, but the will of Him who sent Me. This is the will of Him who sent Me, that of all that He has given Me I lose nothing, but raise it up on the last day (John 6:38-39).

Most of those around Him at the time didn't realize He was completing His Father's wishes to be the utmost sacrifice, and that the act of baptism was Christ's way of showing us what He wanted us to do to remember Him and confirm our life into His cause. Almighty God confirmed at that point that this truly was His beloved Son, and that He was well pleased at Jesus' act of baptism.

This simple act or semblance of what Jesus went through for us is confirmation of obedience and required to cleanse our consciences. I would ask you here: is your conscience clean?

There is no other physical act given in the New Testament which has been mandated as a prerequisite for remission of sin and receiving the gift of the Holy Spirit outside of the laying on of hands by the Apostles. (the Spiritual act is Believing) 2 Corinthians 1:**22** "And he has sealed us and he has given the down payment of his Spirit into our hearts".

Hearing and confession can even be done in one's heart. Even by the deaf and those who can't speak, since they are from the heart, they are also spiritual acts. He that believes shall be saved, and that belief encapsulates the act of baptism just as it incorporates hearing, repentance, confession, obedience, works, faith, a prayer life, worship of the Father, and total submission to His cause. The Bible also teaches us that if we add or take away from the all-inclusive word that we sin, and the truth is not in us.

If we obey the Lord Jesus Christ, we will receive a reward of the inheritance in the Kingdom of Almighty God. We will share in His glory there (Colossians 3:24-25).

When we are baptized (immersed) into Him, we are raised with Him through the faith of the operation of God who raised Jesus from the dead (Colossians 2:12). Being dead in our sins, Jesus quickens us together with Him and forgives us all our trespasses. God the Father, Christ (the Word), the Holy Spirit, and man and woman all share in the Godhead Bodily if we are believers. If I grieve the Holy Spirit, I am not worthy to be the temple He seeks to dwell in (1 Corinthians 6:19). "What? Know ye not that your body is the temple of the Holy Ghost which is in you, which ye have of God, and ye are not your own?"

I can conclude that observing any holiday such as the Epiphany Frost can indeed possibly be a dangerous thing to do. To some it is a hard thing to understand; for me, however, it has become more than a holiday. It is an everyday remembrance of how important my personal baptism was, and I am so thankful I understand why Jesus did it, as well. We don't have to let issues like this one lead us into despair and destruction, as 2 Peter 3:16 has said it will do if I let it. You have enough knowledge to go forward with the act (baptism) and let the Comforter in and accept the remission of your sin (Galatians 4:9-11).

We have learned that Satan has the power to hide the Gospel from those who do not believe and are lost. It is our responsibility to help those who are lost and do not believe (2 Corinthians 4:3-4).

The path of truth or the path of error! There are no middle or outside pathways. Jesus is the Way, the truth, and the life, and no one will enter the Kingdom of Heaven without going through Him.

I cannot separate belief and baptism any more than I can separate the Father, the Son, and the Holy Spirit (James 2:19).

Thou believest that there is one God; thou doest well: the devils also believe, and tremble. (The demons, however, are not obedient to the call of Christ, nor to putting on the character of Christ).

I have heard of cases where so-called Christians don't believe in the Holy Spirit. They simply refuse to take in the all-inclusiveness of the New Testament if they claim that the Holy Spirit is not necessary in their life. We are commanded to be baptized in the name of the Father, the Son, and the Holy Spirit. So how can those who preach that a prayer of faith will make you born again totally ignore the fact that Jesus told Nicodemus that you must be born of the water and the Spirit to be born again?

Don't be misled by the masses! There are multitudes of people preaching false doctrine, and to be a part of that group could lead you to hell! Fast!

I think of it this way. If my God and Creator told me plainly, "call no man father" because there is only one Father in Heaven, and He expects that form of reverence from His children, then no other man should get it. Why would I blatantly deny Him that privilege?

For example: Matthew 23:1-12; Mark 12:38-40; Luke 20:45-47:

> But you are not to be called "rabbi," for you have only one master and you are all brothers. And do not call anyone on Earth "father," for you have one Father, and He is in Heaven. Nor are you to be called "teacher," for you have one teacher, the Christ.

> The greatest among you will be your servant. For whoever exalts himself will be humbled, and whoever humbles himself will be exalted.

Words right out of the Bible, and yet look how millions of people are disobeying God's holy and righteous commands within the denominational world. They are either blatantly denying Christ's commands, or simply have not been taught or read the gospel writings. Perhaps there are so many taking man's word in the man-made creeds and refusing to take the New Testament and study it themselves, thus putting their faith in the wrong place in their lives.

I cannot associate myself with any "religion" that practices calling a man father, rabbi, or teacher, and furthermore who requires that I bow down too or bless their leaders in his presence. Those people are following in the footsteps of Satan himself. The leaders are the blind leading the blind.

John 4:23

> But the hour cometh, and now is, when the true worshippers shall worship the Father in spirit and in truth: for the Father seeketh such to worship Him.

John 4:24

> God is a Spirit: and they that worship Him must
> worship Him in spirit and in truth.

Jesus had this to say to those who taught false religion, and it doesn't
sound like He was whispering, either. See Matthew 23:13-15 and
again in Matthew 23:16-22:

> Woe to you teachers of the law and Pharisees, you
> hypocrites! You shut the Kingdom of Heaven in
> men's faces. You yourselves do not enter, nor will
> you let those enter who are trying to.

> Woe to you teachers of the law and Pharisees, you
> hypocrites! You travel over land and sea to win a
> single convert, and when he becomes one, you make
> him twice as much a son of hell as you are.

> Woe to you, blind guides! You say, if anyone swears
> by the temple, it means nothing: but if anyone
> swears by the gold of the temple, he is bound by his
> oath. You blind fools! Which is greater: the gold or
> the temple that makes the gold sacred?

So how bad is it in our society? Just last night I heard a major TV
journalist call the Pope "Holy Father." Do I think Almighty God was
joking in the book of Matthew, chapter 23? I don't believe so!

Satan called God a liar by telling Adam and Eve they "surely would
not die by partaking of the forbidden fruit, but really they would
be opened up to new understanding and be like God." If you give
reverence to a man by calling him Father or Holy Father, you are
calling God a liar because He said simply "don't do it." If you observe
a holiday in the name of your culture, and have doubts in your belief

to do so, it is sin, because He sent the divinely inspired writers' wisdom which said it could be a dangerous thing to do! I chose to simply not observe it.

Preaching is both foolishness and the power of God (1 Corinthians 1:17-25).

Why should a Christian stay away from all of those "religious organizations" that claim their creeds are plans of salvation? Because the Scripture says so! In the later part of Matthew 15:1-9, and Mark 7:1-13, when Jesus was about 29 years old He said this: "Thus you nullify the Word of God by your tradition that you have handed down. And you do many things like that." Traditions of men and creeds do in fact cause strife and contentions.

I must avoid anyone who causes strife concerning the doctrine of Christ (Romans 16:17).

God is a God of second chances. He is also a God of long suffering; however, He is not forever suffering. That means that there once was a time when He winked at my ignorance, but now He commands obedience because I have gained knowledge and understanding of His Word.

He told us that if we do not produce fruit, the Kingdom will be taken away from us and given to someone who will (Luke 20:17-18; Mark 12:10-11; Matthew 21:42-44). So, if you have been roaming the halls of the church building and have never put on Christ in baptism, here is your chance to change. Find a body of believers who practice what God expects, and then take His Word for what it says. Don't be apathetic about it (Romans 11:23).

If I know to obey the calling to be baptized and I don't do it, I am not only denying Christ, I am not even His friend, much less a member of His Kingdom.

I am only a friend to Jesus if I obey His commandments (John 15:10-27).

If I deny my family the command to be baptized, I will not be reminded of the promises God has given as an inheritance into the Kingdom of Christ. Why, you ask? You cannot be reminded if you don't have the Comforter at your disposal. It is stated that the Holy Spirit is the one who guides us. The Holy Spirit is the down payment that you have the right to inherit the Kingdom once you believe (Ephesians 1:13).

John 1:12

> In whom ye also trusted, after that ye heard the word of truth, the Gospel of your salvation: in whom also after that ye believed, ye were sealed with that Holy Spirit of promise.

> But as many as received Him, to them gave the power (the right to become) the sons of God, even to them that believe on His name.

Your promise of the Comforter is fulfilled when you complete the act of baptism (Acts 2:38).

> Then Peter said unto them, repent, and be baptized every one of you in the name of Jesus Christ for the remission of sins, and ye shall receive the gift of the Holy Ghost.

That is the case unless you were an apostle and had been given the gift by laying-on of hands.

Here is a statement that is sad, which was made after asking a Pharisee who in the parable of the two sons did what his father wanted:

Matthew 21:28-32

> Jesus said to them, I tell you the truth, the tax
> collectors and the prostitutes are entering the
> Kingdom of God ahead of you. For John came to
> you to show you the way of righteousness, and you
> did not believe him, but the tax collectors and the
> prostitutes did. And even after you saw this you did
> not repent and believe him.

Here is a simple way to get a grip on the big picture of baptism. The
following scriptures go hand in hand. Take a pen and paper and
write the scripture and the wording out. Sit back and read it out loud
to yourself (Galatians 3:27; John 14:26; Acts 2:28; Mark 16:15-16;
Romans 6:3-14; Romans 4:15; I Peter 3:21; Acts 10:48).

Do you get the big picture now? Not only is this evidence of a
command, it provides examples.

The steps of submission are not hard, they are just too easy. We as
humans expect things to be hard, and they are not. We just have
a hard time accepting the easy way and create chaos in doing so.
Therefore, there are so many man-made creeds. If God had wanted
additional creeds and traditions of man included in the Gospel,
don't you think He, being the Creator, would have simply just added
another book to the Bible? Maybe He would have called it "Creeds
and Traditions of Men: Requirements for Salvation." Ha! Ha!!

God told us He is a jealous God. He wants it to be His way and His
way only. He told us the way: Jesus is the way, the truth, and the life.
Not *a* way, *a* truth and *a* life! The only way!

Understand this: there will be a time when "all things will be
renewed." Life and existence as we know it now will be different.

Anyone who forsakes this material life for Christ in the unknown, which is in the Kingdom of Heaven, will receive a hundred times as much and will inherit eternal life. But there is one thing to remember, that many who are first will be last, and many who are last will be first (Matthew 19:27-30; Mark 10:28-31; Luke 18:28-30).

I am a sinner; I pray that God will forgive me of my trespasses. I know that He has told me that there is more rejoicing in Heaven over one sinner who repents than over ninety-nine righteous persons who do not need to repent (Luke 15:1-7).

I know there is rejoicing in the presence of the angels of God over one sinner who repents (Luke 15:8-10).

It is recorded that the Jews asked Jesus several times: "If you are the Christ, tell us plainly." Jesus answered, in John 10:22-30:

> I did tell you, but you do not believe. The miracles I do in my Father's name speak for me, but you do not believe because you are not my sheep. My sheep listen to my voice: I know them, and they follow me. I give them eternal life, and they shall never perish: no one can snatch them out of my hand. My Father, who has given them to me, is greater than all, no one can snatch them out of my Father's hand. I and the Father are one.

Jesus, we think, was about 29 years old at that time.

Jesus saw Satan fall from Heaven when he exalted himself and gave up the status of a cherubim angel (Luke 10:17-20). Jesus came to destroy the power Satan gained as the prince of the power of the air here on Earth. Jesus came to destroy death as we know it in the physical body.

Jesus came to give life and more abundantly, exceeding above and beyond what we can imagine if we believe Him.

No one knows who the Son is except the Father, and no one knows who the Father is except the Son, and those to whom the Son chooses to reveal Him (Matthew 25:11-27; Luke 10:21-24).

CHAPTER 8

WHEN DARKNESS REIGNS

Just minutes before Jesus was arrested, He made a statement to those who had come to take Him away. These people included the chief priest, officers of the temple guard, and elders of the church. Jesus asked them, "Am I leading a rebellion that you have come with swords and clubs? Every day I was with you in the temple courts, and you did not lay a hand on me. But this is your hour, when darkness reigns."

Jesus told the disciples that He could have called on God, and He would have sent twelve legions of angels to defend Him. However, this was as the Scriptures said it would happen. Jesus would be betrayed and placed in the hands of murderers. Jesus had just spent hours praying for himself, His disciples, and then for all believers. In John 17:1-5 He asks God to glorify Him in His presence with the glory He had with God before the world began, when Jesus existed in the form of the Word spoken long before He spent 33 years in the physical body of a man.

He prayed in John 17:6-19 for the disciples, that they were the ones God gave Him, and that Jesus had given the words to them that God wanted, and that glory had come to Jesus through the disciple's obedience. He asked God to protect them, only one had been lost and doomed and stated that the world had hated them, and He wanted

God to sanctify them by the word of truth. Jesus ended that prayer by saying that "for the disciples He sanctified himself, that they too may be truly sanctified."

Jesus symbolically sanctified Himself when He had John baptize Him, and spiritually when He died on the cross, was buried and rose again, and ascended into Heaven to be at God's right hand. It is interesting to note that when Jesus "come up out of the water" after his immersion is the only time in the New Testament that all parties of the Godhead Bodily were visually and verbally presented before men!

Matthew 3:13-17

> Then cometh Jesus from Galilee to Jordan unto John, to be baptized of him.[14] But John forbad Him, saying, I have need to be baptized of thee, and comest thou to me?[15] And Jesus answering said unto him, suffer it to be so now: for thus it becometh us to fulfil all righteousness. Then He suffered him.[16] And Jesus, when He was baptized, went up straightway out of the water: and, lo, the heavens were opened unto Him, and He saw the Spirit of God descending like a dove, and lighting upon Him:[17] And lo a voice from Heaven, saying, this is my beloved Son, in whom I am well pleased.

In John 17:20-26, Jesus prayed for all of us believers who trusted in the message of the disciples, that all of us would become one just like Jesus and God and the Holy Spirit are one, and that the world will believe that God sent Jesus. He told God in the prayer that He had given us glory just as God had given Him glory, and asked God to help us to be brought to complete unity to let the world know that indeed God did send Jesus and that God loves us just as He loved Jesus.

He also told God that He wanted us to be with Jesus where He is, and to be able to see His glory, which glory God gave Him because He loved Him before the creation of the world. This is the last statement of prayer we know of before His arrest:

> Righteous Father, though the world does not know you, I know you, and they know that you have sent me. I have made you known to them and will continue to make you known in order that the love you have for me may be in them and that I myself may be in them.

If we go backward in time just before these three prayers, we find something most interesting. In John 16:12-15, Jesus gives His followers important information concerning the Holy Spirit's guidance: "I have much more to say to you, more than you can now bear."

> But when He, the Spirit of Truth, comes, He will guide you into all truth. He will not speak on His own; He will speak only what He hears, and He will tell you what is yet to come. He will bring glory to me by taking from what is mine and making it known to you. All that belongs to the Father is mine. That is why I said the Spirit will take from what is mine and make it known to you.

Here we see and understand that without the Holy Spirit in our lives, we cannot know what is to come, nor be made aware of all that belongs to the Father which is made known to those who believe.

Also, in John 16:5-11 Jesus says:

> But I tell you the truth: it is for your good that I am going away. Unless I go away, the Counselor will not come to you; but if I go, I will send Him to

you. When He comes, He will convict the world of guilt regarding sin and righteousness and judgment; regarding sin, because men do not believe in me; regarding righteousness, because I am going to the Father, where you can see me no longer; and regarding judgment, because the prince of this world now stands condemned.

Verification that Satan is doomed is now being released by the one who brings him condemnation. The world is now convicted of sin by the gift of the Counselor (Holy Spirit) regarding sin, righteousness, and judgment. Remember what the Bible said about repenting, confessing, and being baptized for the remission of sin, and you shall receive the gift of the Holy Spirit (the Comforter).

Continuing with **John 15:18 through 16-4**:

In these verses we are taught that Jesus knew the mentality of those who would terrorize us, and that they are the antichrist because they simply do not believe in Him.

If the world hates you, keep in mind that it hated me first.

If they persecuted me, they will persecute you also.

If I had not come and spoken to them, they would not be guilty of sin. Now, however, they have no excuse for their sin. He who hates me hates my Father as well. If I had not done among them what no one else did, they would not be guilty of sin.

But now they have seen these miracles, and yet they have hated both me and my Father. But this is to fulfill what is written in their law: they hated me without reason.

They will put you out of the synagogue (assembly); in fact, a time is coming when anyone who kills you will think he is offering a service to God. (Extremist mentality today)

I think of it this way: They are just breathing the ashes of their master's wings! Satan got his wings burned off when he was hurled down from Heaven like a lightning bolt. Now he crawls! They (satan's followers) have no control over their lust to destroy us, because they are consumed by guilt. They pretend to be light, but they are darkness. Their angel now is on his belly; he has no arms or legs, much less any wings now. He is doomed, and he wants to take all he can to his future home, the Abyss!

ASHES OF AN ANGEL'S WINGS

They wish they had my angel, because I'm so blessed
For just one true moment of love
It's a wish in their darkness,
Which they will never rise above
Deep into their dying day, waiting for the noose
They take a step into a light, turn into dust
Burning, going down frail and loose
In their angel's arms full of lust
So young, life's just an escape from this world
Join them in death is the song they sing
Trading lives for one moment, one swirl
Breathing in the ashes of an angel's wings
They wish they had my angel, just to destroy
In their eyes a true moment of love
Just a wish in their darkness, a decoy

Stained they will never rise above
Everything is death to them, a desire
No matter any more or less
Night falls, their fallen angel is on fire
They lose the fight against the darkness
So young, life's just an escape from this world
Join them in death is the song they sing
Trading lives for one moment, one swirl
Breathing in the ashes of an angel's wings
So, life escaped, they never knew the score
Death took them, a song they had to sing
Trading lives for one moment, just one breath more
Breathing in the ashes of a fallen angel's wings

John 15:18 through 16-4:

They will do such things because they have not known the Father or me, I have told you this, so that when the time comes you will remember that I warned you. I did not tell you this at first because I was with you.

These statements are from the Savior, recorded almost 2,000 years ago, and it is exactly what is happening today. All extreme terror comes from the antichrist mentality because they don't know the Father and they hate both God and Jesus. They are children of their father, the devil.

The time has come that those who do these acts think they are offering a service to God. All of those who terrorize are guilty of sin, because Jesus did in fact come and perform miracles. Jesus chose not to tell us these things when He was here on Earth with us. He did it for a reason. At the time He was preparing His disciples for His persecution. In Revelation 21:6-8, those cowards are called unbelieving, vile, murderers, sexually immoral, practices of magical arts, idolaters and liars.

There was only so much the disciples could comprehend at that time. He even said in John 16:12, "I have much more to say to you, more than you can now bear." Jesus gave the exact forewarning of what would happen in our society today, just before He was arrested.

There are many more predictions which Jesus foretold, such as in Matthew 24:4-35; Mark 13:5-31; Luke 21:8-33.

> Watch out that no one deceives you. For many will come in my name, claiming, 'I am the Christ,' and will deceive many. You will hear of wars and rumors of wars but see to it that you are not alarmed. Such things must happen, but the end is still to come.

He goes on to tell of the forthcoming events which happened in 70 AD regarding the destruction of the Temple in Jerusalem, and differentiates between that event and the Second Coming.

In Matthew 24:36-44 and Mark 13:32-33 he makes it known that "no one knows the day or hour when the Son of Man will come, not even the angels in Heaven, nor the Son (Jesus), but only the Father knows." We are told to just keep watch, be ready, because the Son of Man will come at an hour when you do not expect Him.

Revelation 22:12-16

A message for fallen Christians: "All people have disobeyed God, and that's why He treats them as prisoners, but He does this so that He can have mercy on all of them" (Romans 11:32).

If those other branches will start having faith, they will be made a part of that tree again. God has the power to put them back. After all, it wasn't natural for branches to be cut from a wild olive tree. So, it is much more likely that God will join the natural branches back to the cultivated olive tree (Romans 11:23-24).

So! Can you fall from grace? Absolutely! Even angels can.

Can you be fully restored into God's Kingdom once you have fallen? Absolutely! But only if it is God's will,

Who can measure the wealth and the wisdom of God? Who can understand His decisions or explain what He does? (Romans 11:33)

CHAPTER 9

DYING SPIRITUALLY

2 Corinthians 4:1-6

Ours is a straightforward ministry bringing light into darkness:

> This is the ministry of the new agreement which
> God in His mercy has given us and nothing can
> daunt us. We use no hocus-pocus, no clever tricks,
> and no dishonest manipulation of the Word of God.
> We speak the plain truth and so commend ourselves
> to every man's conscience in the sight of God. If our
> Gospel is "veiled," the veil must be in the minds of
> those who are "spiritually dying." The spirit of this
> world has blinded the minds of those who do not
> believe and prevents the light of the glorious Gospel
> of Christ, the image of God, from shining on them.
> For it is Christ Jesus the Lord whom we preach,
> not ourselves; we are your servants for His sake.
> God, who first ordered 'light to shine in darkness,'
> has flooded our hearts with His light. We now
> can enlighten men only because we can give them
> knowledge of the glory of God, as we see it in the
> face of Jesus Christ.

What power does the "spirit of this world" who has blinded so many now have?

Ephesians 2:2

> Wherein in time past ye walked according to the course of this world, according to the prince of the power of the air, the spirit that now worketh in the children of disobedience.

Revelation 20:2

> And He laid hold on the dragon, that old serpent, which is the Devil, and Satan, and bound him a thousand years.

2 Corinthians 11:13

> For such are false apostles, deceitful workers, transforming themselves into the apostles of Christ. [12]How art thou fallen from Heaven, O Lucifer, son of the morning! How art thou cut down to the ground, which didst weaken the nations! [13]For thou hast said in thine heart, I will ascend into Heaven, I will exalt my throne above the stars of God: I will sit also upon the mount of the congregation, in the sides of the north: [14]I will ascend above the heights of the clouds; I will be like the most High. [15]Yet thou shalt be brought down to hell, to the sides of the pit.

John 12:31

> Now is the time for judgment on this world; now the prince of this world will be driven out.

John 14:30

> I will not say much more to you, for the prince of
> this world is coming. He has no hold over me.

John 16:11

> And about judgment, because the prince of this
> world now stands condemned.

The spiritually dead are those who are carnally minded instead of
spiritually minded.

Romans 8:6

> For to be carnally minded is death; but to be
> spiritually minded is life and peace.

Romans 8:7

> Because the carnal mind is enmity against God: for
> it is not subject to the law of God, neither indeed
> can be.

Romans 6:11

> Likewise reckon ye also yourselves to be dead indeed
> unto sin, but alive unto God through Jesus Christ
> our Lord.

I inherited a carnal mind through the sins of Adam and Eve, but
in Christ I inherit life eternal and become a new spiritual-minded
person. This is called "being made alive," or a rebirth.

1 Corinthians 15:22

For as in Adam all die, even so in Christ shall all be made alive.

Jesus Christ (the Word) became flesh and left the glory of Heaven to bring salvation unto all men in form of a man. Once He fulfilled His mission, He returned into His original glory at the right hand of Almighty God and then He sent the Comforter (the Holy Spirit) to guide us as we live our lives in Him.

John 1:1

In the beginning was the Word, and the Word was with God, and the Word was God. *[The Word Became Flesh]*

John 1:14

The Word became flesh and made His dwelling among us. We have seen His glory, the glory of the one and only Son, who came from the Father, full of grace and truth.

Matthew 1:18

Now the birth of Jesus Christ was on this wise: when as His mother Mary was espoused to Joseph, before they came together, she was found with child of the Holy Ghost.

John 14:16

And I will pray the Father, and He shall give you another Comforter, that He may abide with you forever.

John 14:26

But the Comforter, which is the Holy Ghost, whom the Father will send in my name, He shall teach you all things, and bring all things to your remembrance, whatsoever I have said unto you.

God the Father, God the Son, and God the Comforter (Holy Spirit) are one in the same being called the Godhead Bodily.

Acts 17:29

Forasmuch then as we are the offspring of God, we ought not to think that the Godhead is like unto gold, or silver, or stone, graven by art and man's device.

Romans 1:20

For the invisible things of Him from the creation of the world are clearly seen, being understood by the things that are made, even His eternal power and Godhead; so that they are without excuse.

Colossians 2:9

For in Him (Jesus) dwelleth all the fullness of the Godhead Bodily.

Who could keep our Savior from returning to His original glory after such exceeding wonderful kindness to redeem us back to His Father? This was His mission, to give His life for us (become the propitiation for our sins) and return to His original glory!

Luke 24:26

> Ought not Christ to have suffered these things, and to enter His glory?

Romans 3:25

> Whom God hath set forth to be a propitiation (sacrifice) through faith in His blood, to declare His righteousness for the remission of sins that are past, through the forbearance of God.

1 John 2:2

> And He is the propitiation (sacrifice) for our sins: and not for ours only, but also for the sins of the whole world.

1 John 4:10

> Herein is love, not that we loved God, but that He loved us, and sent His Son to be the propitiation (sacrifice) for our sins.

What will Christ do now that He has returned to His glory?

John 14:2

> My Father's house has many rooms; if that were not so, would I have told you that I am going there to prepare a place for you?

John 11:27

> She saith unto him, Yea, Lord: I believe that thou art the Christ, the Son of God, which should come into the world.

Romans 6:3

> Know ye not, that so many of us as were baptized into Jesus Christ were baptized into His death?

Romans 6:4

> Therefore we are buried with Him by baptism into death: that like as Christ was raised up from the dead by the glory of the Father, even so we also should walk in newness of life.

Romans 10:6

> But the righteousness which is of faith speaketh on this wise, say not in thine heart, who shall ascend into Heaven? *(That is, to bring Christ down from above.)*

Romans 10:7

> Or, who shall descend into the deep? *(That is, to bring up Christ again from the dead.)*

Why should we remind our brothers and sisters in Christ and encourage, admonish and exhort each other, no matter how sinful we are? Why would God use such people as me (a sinner), as the Apostle Paul (a murderer), as the woman at the well (an adulteress), to bring our loved ones into remembrance of the ways of Christ?

1 Corinthians 4:17

> For this cause have I sent unto you Timotheus, who is my beloved son, and faithful in the Lord, who shall bring you into remembrance of my ways which be in Christ, as I teach everywhere in every church.

2 Corinthians 10:5

> Casting down imaginations, and every high thing that exalteth itself against the knowledge of God and bringing into captivity every thought to the obedience of Christ.

Perhaps to help us discern who is of God and who is of Satan, the great deceiver.

2 Corinthians 11:13

> For such are false apostles, deceitful workers, transforming themselves into the apostles of Christ.

Matthew 7:15

> Beware of false prophets, which come to you in sheep's clothing, but inwardly they are ravening wolves.

Matthew 24:11

> And many false prophets shall rise and shall deceive many.

Matthew 24:24

> For there shall arise false Christs, and false prophets, and shall shew great signs and wonders; insomuch that, if it were possible, they shall deceive the very elect.

Mark 13:22

> For false Christs and false prophets shall rise, and shall shew signs and wonders, to seduce, if it were possible, even the elect.

Luke 6:26

> Woe unto you, when all men shall speak well of you! For so did their fathers to the false prophets.

2 Peter 2:1

> But there were false prophets also among the people, even as there shall be false teachers among you, who privily shall bring in damnable heresies, even denying the Lord that bought them, and bringing upon themselves swift destruction.

1 John 4:1

> Beloved, believe not every spirit, but try the spirits whether they are of God: because many false prophets are gone out into the world.

Proof that all blinded unbelievers are antichrist, not just one!

2 Corinthians 4:1-6

> Therefore, since through God's mercy we have this ministry, we do not lose heart. [2]Rather, we have renounced secret and shameful ways; we do not use deception, nor do we distort the Word of God. On the contrary, by setting forth the truth plainly we commend ourselves to everyone's conscience in the sight of God. [3]And even if our Gospel is veiled, it is veiled to those who are perishing. [4]The god of this age has blinded the minds of unbelievers, so that they cannot see the light of the Gospel that displays the glory of Christ, who is the image of God. [5]For what we preach is not ourselves, but Jesus Christ as Lord, and ourselves as your servants for Jesus' sake. [6]For God, who said, "Let light shine out of darkness," [a]made His light shine in our hearts to give us the light of the knowledge of God's glory displayed in the face of Christ.

A warning against denying that Jesus came in the flesh!

1 John 2:18

> Dear children, this is the last hour; and as you have heard that the antichrist is coming, even now many antichrists have come. This is how we know it is the last hour.

2 John 1:7

> I say this because many deceivers, who do not acknowledge Jesus Christ as coming in the flesh, have gone out into the world. Any such person is the deceiver and the antichrist.

CHAPTER 10

DESIRING THE FIRE

2 Peter 3:10-12

> [10]But the day of the Lord will come like a thief. The heavens will disappear with a roar; the elements will be destroyed by fire, and the Earth and everything done in it will be laid bare. [11]since everything will be destroyed in this way, what kind of people ought you to be? You ought to live holy and godly lives [12]as you look forward to the day of God and speed its coming. That day will bring about the destruction of the heavens by fire, and the elements will melt in the heat.

What is the word here for fire?

The verb *kausoo* is used for the future destruction of the natural elements in 2 Peter 3:10, 12, "with fervent heat," in the passive voice, "being burned."

2 Peter 3:10-12

> But the day of the Lord will come as a thief in the night; in which the heavens shall pass away with a

great noise, and the elements shall melt with fervent heat, the Earth also and the works that are therein shall be burned up. [11]Seeing then that all these things shall be dissolved, what manner of persons ought ye to be in all holy conversation and godliness, [12]looking for and hasting unto the coming of the day of God, wherein the heavens being on fire shall be dissolved, and the elements shall melt with fervent heat?

What are elements?

The Greek word *stoicheion* is used in the sense of the substance of the material world, 2 Peter 3:10, 12.

What does it mean to be hasting or haste, with haste, hastily?

The Greek verb *pseudo* means "to desire earnestly," 2 Peter 3:12, RV, "earnestly desiring."

So! As a Christian I am told to "earnestly desire" and look forward to the day in which our world as we know it (materially) will be dissolved in fervent heat. What is left then?

1 Corinthians 3

Brothers and sisters, I could not address you as people who live by the Spirit but as people who are still worldly—mere infants in Christ. [2]I gave you milk, not solid food, for you were not yet ready for it. Indeed, you are still not ready. [3]You are still worldly. For since there is jealousy and quarreling among you, are you not worldly? Are you not acting like mere humans? [4]For when one says, "I follow Paul," and another, "I follow Apollos," are you not mere human beings?

⁵What, after all, is Apollos? And what is Paul? Only servants through whom you came to believe as the Lord has assigned to each his task. ⁶I planted the seed, Apollos watered it, but God has been making it grow. ⁷So neither the one who plants nor the one who waters is anything, but only God, who makes things grow. ⁸The one who plants and the one who waters have one purpose, and they will each be rewarded according to their own labor. ⁹For we are co-workers in God's service; you are God's field, God's building.

¹⁰By the grace God has given me, I laid a foundation as a wise builder, and someone else is building on it. But each one should build with care. ¹¹For no one can lay any foundation other than the one already laid, which is Jesus Christ. ¹²If anyone builds on this foundation using gold, silver, costly stones, wood, hay or straw, **¹³their work will be shown for what it is, because the day will bring it to light. It will be revealed with fire, and the fire will test the quality of each person's work. ¹⁴If what has been built survives, the builder will receive a reward. ¹⁵If it is burned up, the builder will suffer loss but yet will be saved—even though only as one escaping through the flames.**

¹⁶Don't you know that you yourselves are God's temple and that God's Spirit dwells in your midst? ¹⁷If anyone destroys God's temple, God will destroy that person; for God's temple is sacred, and you together are that temple.

¹⁸Do not deceive yourselves. If any of you think you are wise by the standards of this age, you should

become "fools" so that you may become wise. [19]For the wisdom of this world is foolishness in God's sight. As it is written: "He catches the wise in their craftiness," [a] [20]and again, "The Lord knows that the thoughts of the wise are futile." [b] [21]So then, no more boasting about human leaders! All things are yours, [22]whether Paul or Apollos or Cephas[c] or the world or life or death or the present or the future—all are yours, [23]and you are of Christ, and Christ is of God.

Yes! You yourselves are God's temple, if you are called. Almighty God's spirit dwells inside of you. We are instructed not to destroy our body because God uses us for a dwelling place for His Holy Spirit to reside. Our bodies are sacred to God and we need to understand that if we destroy our flesh, God will destroy us.

This is what is left after the fire:

- The souls of men who are spiritual.
- Those who share in the Godhead Bodily.
- Those who are one with Christ, the Holy Spirit and God the Father.
- Those who "together" make up God's temple.
- Those spiritual beings (workers) who have proven their faith by what they did while on Earth in rightly handling the word of truth.
- True disciples of Christ will remain after the Great Fire and are those who are not ashamed to suffer as one who carries the name of Christ and glorifies God in so doing.

1 Peter 4:16

However, if you suffer as a Christian, do not be ashamed, but praise God that you bear that name.

Evidence that faith without works is dead.

James 2

14What good is it, my brothers and sisters, if someone claims to have faith but has no deeds? Can such faith save them? 15Suppose a brother or a sister is without clothes and daily food. 16If one of you says to them, "Go in peace; keep warm and well fed," but does nothing about their physical needs, what good is it? 17In the same way, faith by itself, if it is not accompanied by action, is dead.

18But someone will say, "You have faith; I have deeds." Show me your faith without deeds, and I will show you my faith by my deeds. 19You believe that there is one God. Good! Even the demons believe that—and shudder.

20You foolish person, do you want evidence that faith without deeds is useless? [d] 21Was not our father Abraham considered righteous for what he did when he offered his son Isaac on the altar? 22You see that his faith and his actions were working together, and his faith was made complete by what he did. 23And the Scripture was fulfilled that says, "Abraham believed God, and it was credited to him as righteousness," and he was called God's friend. 24You see that a person is considered righteous by what they do and not by faith alone.

25In the same way, was not even Rahab the prostitute considered righteous for what she did when she gave lodging to the spies and sent them off in a different direction? [26]As the body without the spirit is dead, so faith without deeds is dead.

2 Timothy 2:15

Do your best to present yourself to God as one approved, a worker who does not need to be ashamed and who correctly handles the word of truth.

What pattern of teaching do I allow to claim my allegiance?

Romans 6

Dead to Sin, Alive in Christ

[1]What shall we say, then? Shall we go on sinning so that grace may increase? [2]By no means! We are those who have died to sin; how can we live in it any longer? [3]Or don't you know that all of us who were baptized into Christ Jesus were baptized into His death? [4]We were therefore buried with Him through baptism into death in order that, just as Christ was raised from the dead through the glory of the Father, we too may live a new life.

[5]For if we have been united with Him in a death like His, we will certainly also be united with Him in a resurrection like His. [6]For we know that our old self was crucified with Him so that the body ruled by sin might be done away with that we should no longer be slaves to sin— [7]because anyone who has died has been set free from sin.

[8]Now if we died with Christ, we believe that we will also live with Him. [9]For we know that since Christ

was raised from the dead, He cannot die again; death no longer has mastery over Him. [10]The death He died, He died to sin once for all; but the life He lives, He lives to God.

[11]In the same way, count yourselves dead to sin but alive to God in Christ Jesus. [12]Therefore do not let sin reign in your mortal body so that you obey its evil desires. [13]Do not offer any part of yourself to sin as an instrument of wickedness, but rather offer yourselves to God as those who have been brought from death to life; and offer every part of yourself to Him as an instrument of righteousness. [14]For sin shall no longer be your master, because you are not under the law, but under grace.

Slaves to Righteousness

[15]What then? Shall we sin because we are not under the law but under grace? By no means! [16]Don't you know that when you offer yourselves to someone as obedient slaves, you are slaves of the one you obey— whether you are slaves to sin, which leads to death, or to obedience, which leads to righteousness? [17]But thanks be to God that, though you used to be slaves to sin, you have come to obey from your heart the pattern of teaching that has now claimed your allegiance. [18]You have been set free from sin and have become slaves to righteousness.

[19]I am using an example from everyday life because of your human limitations. Just as you used to offer yourselves as slaves to impurity and to ever-increasing wickedness, so now offer yourselves as slaves to righteousness leading to holiness. [20]When

you were slaves to sin, you were free from the control of righteousness. [21]What benefit did you reap at that time from the things you are now ashamed of? Those things result in death! [22]But now that you have been set free from sin and have become slaves of God, the benefit you reap leads to holiness, and the result is eternal life. [23]For the wages of sin is death, but the gift of God is eternal life in [b]Christ Jesus our Lord.

How do I become set free from sin?

- Hear this Word!
- Believe it! (receive the down payment, the Seal of the Holy Spirit)
- Confess it!
- Repent (change)!
- Be baptized into Christ (receive remission of sin and the gift of the holy spirit in doing so)!
- Remain obedient to His commandments!
- Prove your faith by your works! (Build up your Rewards in Heaven)
- Share this truth! (fulfill your obligation to reconcile others back to God) 2 Corinthians 5:18

CHAPTER 11

HOW TO PLAN A LIFE

Plan to not worry! God will provide all you need in this life.

Matthew 6:34

> Take therefore no thought for the morrow: for the morrow shall take thought for the things of itself. Enough unto the day is the evil thereof.

Plan to ask God for what you want, "if it be His will."

Philippians 4:6

> Be careful about nothing; but in everything by prayer and supplication with thanksgiving let your requests be made known unto God.

1 John 5:14

God only hears us if we ask according to His will. Ask something of God just because you desire it for selfish reasons, and He probably will not even hear it. If you ask it to be so if it is His will, I am sure He will hear it and answer according to whether it is beneficial to you at the time. God said He would never forsake you or leave you.

You must be the one to have faith that He will do what He said He would do.

Plan to not let the physical things (possessions) rule your life.

1 Timothy 6:7

> For we brought nothing into this world, and it is certain we can carry nothing out.

Plan to live in unity in the Body of Christ!

Jesus prays for all believers:

> [20]My prayer is not for them alone. I pray also for those who will believe in me through their message, [21]that all of them may be one, Father, just as you are in me and I am in you. May they also be in us so that the world may believe that you have sent me. [22]I have given them the glory that you gave me, that they may be one as we are one, [23]I in them and you in me—so that they may be brought to complete unity. Then the world will know that you sent me and have loved them even as you have loved me.

Plan to accomplish everything within the realm of Christianity.

John 15:5

> [5]I am the vine; you are the branches. If you remain in me and I in you, you will bear much fruit; apart from me you can do nothing.

Plan to depend upon God and not what mankind can do to hurt you. Deny the terrorist!

Hebrews 13:6

> So we say with confidence, "The Lord is my helper;
> I will not be afraid. What can mere mortals do
> to me?"

Plan to show mercy to all people and pray for mercy yourself!

James 2:13

Because judgment without mercy will be shown to anyone who has
not been merciful. Mercy triumphs over judgment.

Plan to avoid the pollution and strife of this life.

Revelation 3:4

> Yet you have a few people in Sardis who have not
> soiled their clothes. They will walk with me, dressed
> in white, for they are worthy.

Romans 16:17

> I must avoid anyone who causes strife concerning
> the doctrine of Christ.

Plan to help those less fortunate than you are.

1 Thessalonians 5:14

> And we urge you, brothers and sisters, warn
> those who are idle and disruptive, encourage
> the disheartened, help the weak, be patient with
> everyone.

Plan to avoid those who try to lead you astray.

2 Thessalonians 3:6

> In the name of the Lord Jesus Christ, we command you, brothers and sisters, to keep away from every believer who is idle and disruptive and does not live according to the teaching you received from us. *[warning against idleness]*

Hebrews 2:1

> We must pay the most careful attention, therefore, to what we have heard, so that we do not drift away. *[warning to pay attention]*

Plan to hear the voice of the Holy Spirit.

Hebrews 3:7

> So, as the Holy Spirit says: "Today, if you hear His voice" *[warning against unbelief]*

Plan to fear (reverence) Almighty God and not man.

Hebrews 11:7

> By faith Noah, when warned about things not yet seen, in holy fear built an ark to save his family. By his faith he condemned the world and became heir of the righteousness that is in keeping with faith.

Plan to live in peace with all men as much as you can and still glorify God.

Hebrews 12:14

> Make every effort to live in peace with everyone and
> to be holy; without holiness no one will see the Lord.
> *[warning and encouragement]*

Plan to listen and learn.

Hebrews 12:25

> See to it that you do not refuse him who speaks. If
> they did not escape when they refused Him who
> warned them on Earth, how much less will we, if we
> turn away from Him who warns us from Heaven?

**Plan to never deny Christ as the Son of God and that he is equal
to God and the Holy Spirit.**

1 John 2:18

> Dear children, this is the last hour; and as you have
> heard that the antichrist is coming, even now many
> antichrists have come. This is how we know it is the
> last hour.

Plan to receive a crown of glory when the Lord returns.

Revelation 22:12

> "Look, I am coming soon! My reward is with me,
> and I will give to each person according to what
> they have done.

I am to hope for the things I cannot see with the naked eye.

Romans 5:2

> By whom also we have access by faith into this grace wherein we stand and rejoice in hope of the glory of God.

Colossians 1:27

> Christ in you is your hope of Glory.

Plan on tribulations to come your way and prepare to glory in them—that is how you become a patient person.

Romans 8:24-25

> [24]For in this hope we were saved. But hope that is seen is no hope at all. Who hopes for what they already have? [25]But if we hope for what we do not yet have, we wait for it patiently.

Plan to love your enemies and expect nothing in return.

Luke 6:35

> But love your enemies, and do good, and lend, hoping for nothing again; and your reward shall be great, and ye shall be the children of the Highest: for He is kind unto the unthankful and to the evil.

Plan your life to forgive others so your Heavenly Father will forgive you.

Luke 7:42

> And when they had nothing to pay, He frankly forgave them both. Tell me therefore, which of them will love Him most?

Plan your life like an open book that cannot be hid.

Luke 12:2

> For there is nothing covered, that shall not be revealed; neither hid, that shall not be known.

Luke 8:17

> For nothing is secret, that shall not be made manifest; neither anything hid, that shall not be known and come abroad.

Plan to abide in Christ no matter what hardships may come your way.

John 15:5

> I am the vine, ye are the branches: He that abides in me, and I in Him, the same brings forth much fruit: for without me ye can do nothing.

Plan to be judged by no one except the Lord Himself.

1 Corinthians 4:4

> For I know nothing by myself; yet am I not hereby justified: but he that judges me is the Lord.

Plan your life to share the good news of the Gospel of Christ.

1 Corinthians 9:16

> For though I preach the Gospel, I have nothing to glory of: for necessity is laid upon me; yea, woe is unto me, if I preach not the Gospel!

Plan to change when you realize you're doing wrong.

2 Corinthians 7:9

> Now I rejoice, not that ye were made sorry, but that ye sorrowed to repentance: for ye were made sorry after a godly manner, that ye might receive damage by us in nothing.

Plan to seek out the truth in fear and trembling.

2 Corinthians 13:8

> For we can do nothing against the truth, but for the truth.

See also Galatians 2:5-7

Plan to esteem others more highly than yourself.

Galatians 6:3

> For if a man think himself to be something, when he is nothing, he deceives himself.

Plan to suffer, knowing you will bring God glory and receive glory one day.

Romans 8:18

> For I reckon that the sufferings of this present time are not worthy to be compared with the glory which shall be revealed in us.

> The Creator allows us to suffer a while to make us perfect, establish, strengthen and settle us and to bring Him glory.

1 Peter 4:14-16 and 5:10

Philippians 12:7-30

> It is better for us to suffer for doing well than it is for us to suffer for doing evil.

1 Peter 3:17

Plan to be guided by the Comforter and pray for the Comforter to direct you.

Acts 2:38 says, "Change and be immersed in water, every one of you, in the name of Jesus Christ for the remission of sins, and you will receive the gift of the Comforter."

Acts 2:28: There are two blessings we get when we are immersed into Christ. We are told that remission or release of sin is the first gift, and then second, we receive the Comforter. To get these special blessings, we must hear the Word, believe it, change our attitude toward the Gospel, confess our sins and be baptized in the name of Jesus Christ. Then we must be obedient to this calling.

Steve C. Varner

John 14:16-17

> And Jesus will ask God the Father, and he will give you another Counselor to be with you forever, who is the Spirit of Truth.

John 16:13

> But when the Spirit of Truth comes He will guide us into all truth, however will not speak on His own but will speak only what He hears from God the Father and He will tell you what is yet to come and will bring glory to Jesus by taking from what is Jesus' and making it known to us. All that belongs to the Father is also Jesus'. That is why Jesus said the Spirit will take from what is His and make it known to us.

No man can say that Jesus is the Lord unless he is directed by the Holy Spirit to do so.

1 Corinthians 12:3

> I have a Comforter who will remind me of all of the promises I inherit as a Christian.

John 14:26

Plan to hear God's Word.

John 6:45: Jesus Himself said: "It is written in the prophets, and they shall be all taught of God. Every man therefore that hath heard, and hath learned of the Father, cometh unto me." He goes on to say, "He that believes on me shall have everlasting life."

Plan to believe God's Word.

John 6:45: we are to believe that Jesus is who He said He was, the only begotten Son of God, and that He is God in the flesh.

> For with the heart man believes unto righteousness and with the mouth confession is made unto salvation.

Luke 12:8 KJV

We get strength when we accept or believe in the principle of grace (2 Timothy 2:1).

Satan has the power to hide the Gospel from those who do not believe and are lost. It is our responsibility to help those who are lost and do not believe.

2 Corinthians 4:3-4

Plan to confess your faults to each other.

Romans 10:9-10 KJV

> That if thou shalt confess with thy mouth the Lord Jesus, and shalt believe in thine heart that God hath raised Him from the dead, thou shalt be saved.

> Also, I say unto you, whosoever shall confess me before men, him shall the Son of Man also confess before the angels of God.

Romans 14:11 KJV

> For it is written, as I live, saith the Lord, every knee shall bow to me, and every tongue shall confess to God.

Plan to be baptized for the remission of your sins.

Acts 2:38

> Change and be immersed in water, every one of you, in the name of Jesus Christ for the remission of sins, and you will receive the gift of the Comforter.

Romans 6:3-4, 16-17

> Know you not that so many of us as were baptized (immersed) into Jesus Christ were baptized into His death? Therefore, we are buried with Him by baptism into death. That like as Christ was raised up from the dead by the glory of the Father, even so we also should walk in newness of life. For if we have been planted together in the likeness of His death, we shall be also in the likeness of His resurrection; knowing this, that our old man is crucified with Him, that the body of sin might be destroyed, that henceforth we should not serve sin. For he that is dead is freed from sin.

> Now if we be dead with Christ, we believe that we shall also live with Him. For in that He died, He died unto sin once, but in that He lives, He lives unto God.

> Likewise reckon you also yourselves to be dead indeed unto sin, but alive unto God through Jesus Christ our Lord. For ye are not under the law, but under grace! Sin shall have no dominion over you.

1 Peter 3:21

Yes! Salvation comes by grace and by water.

> The like figure whereunto even baptism does also now save us (not by the putting away of the filth of the flesh), but the answer of a good conscience toward God, by the resurrection of Jesus Christ who is gone into Heaven, and is on the right hand of God, angels and authorities and powers being made subject unto Him.

1 Peter 3:15-22

This is your answer for the reason of the hope within you! Baptism does save us by cleansing our conscience toward God (verse 15) and by the resurrection of Jesus Christ (verse 21).

Plan to obey the commandments set forth, knowing you are going to fail at some.

Hebrews 5:9

> And Christ, fulfilling perfection in His life here on Earth, became the author of eternal salvation unto all them that obey Him.

The gift of grace or wonderful kindness can be taken away from us simply by our disobedience to God's will, even if we once experienced it.

2 Peter 3:17

> I am only a friend to Jesus if I obey His commandments.

John 15:10-27

> I have a place prepared for me in Heaven now if I am obedient to God in His great plan.

John 14:1-3

Plan to do works, not for salvation, but for reward.

Colossians 1:28-29

> We announce the message about Jesus, and we use all our wisdom to warn and teach everyone, so that all of Christ's followers will grow in the spirit and become mature disciples of Christ.

Each man's work shall be made manifest as stated in **1 Corinthians 3:13**.

> For the day shall declare it, because it is revealed in fire! And the fire itself shall prove each man's work of what sort it is [14]if any man's work shall abide which he built thereon, he shall receive a reward. [15]If any man's work shall be burned he shall suffer loss, but he himself shall be saved, yet so as through fire!

So! Our works done here on Earth will be tried in fire, whether good or bad. We will either receive a reward or suffer loss for those works. The salvation of our souls, however, depends upon God.

The moon and stars and Earth, with all the works people do, will melt some day with fervent heat. Right now, it all is just being kept in store reserved unto fire. The first time the Earth was destroyed by water and only a few were saved. The next time God destroys the Earth it will be by fire, and even the firmaments and planets will melt.

2 Peter 3:7-11

There will come a day when God will not only shake the Earth, but He will also shake Heaven.

Hebrews 12:26

The Lord Jesus will take vengeance in flaming fire on all of those who have troubled us as Christians and they will be punished with everlasting destruction from the presence of the Lord. This is a righteous thing with God.

2 Thessalonians 1:6-9

All the works I do while here on Earth will be tried by fire.

1 Corinthians 3:13

Faith without works is dead.

James 2:24-26

Plan to share faith, hope, and love.

Romans 8:24-25

For in unseen hope we are saved, but hope that is seen is no hope at all. Who hopes for what he already has? But if we hope for what we do not yet have, we wait for it patiently.

Romans 8:15, 26

> For we did not receive a spirit that makes us slaves
> again to fear: but we received the spirits of son-ship.

Now we must add to our faith, virtue, temperance, patience, godliness, brotherly kindness, and love.

Plan to be humble in life.

Psalms 34:18 says "The Lord is high unto them that are of a broken heart and saves such as be of a contrite spirit."

1 John 4:15 -21

> Those who confess that Jesus is the Son of God,
> God dwells in him, and he in God. And we have
> known and believed the love that God has for us.
> God is love; and he that dwells in love dwells in God
> and God in him. Herein is our love made perfect,
> that we may have boldness in the Day of Judgment;
> because as He is so are we in this world. There is no
> fear in love; but perfect love casts out fear; because
> fear hath torment. He that fears is not made perfect
> in love. We love Him, because He first loved us. If a
> man says I love God, and hates his brother, he is a
> liar; for he that loves not his brother whom he has
> seen, how can he love God; whom he has not seen?
> And the commandment we have from Him is that
> he who loves God loves his brother also.

Plan to refuse to sit back and do nothing while here on this Earth.

James 5:20

> He who leads another from the error of their ways shall hide a multitude of sins.

Jude 21-23

> Christians! You must stay in the love of God, looking for the mercy of our Lord Jesus Christ unto eternal life. And on some have compassion, making a difference through love; and others save them with fear if necessary, pulling them out of the fire and hating even the garment spotted by the flesh.

Plan on believing in angels.

Psalms 91:11-12

> For God will place His angels in charge over you to keep you sound in the ways of judgment.

Hebrews 1:13-14

> They will guide your feet and keep you from kicking against the stones.

Matthew 24:31, Mark 13:27

> The good angels will gather God's elect people for the Judgment Day.

Plan to be ready to give a reason for the hope that is in you.

1 Peter 3:15

> Always be ready and willing to give a reason of the hope that is inside you.

Psalm 42:11

> Why are you so down and out, my soul? And why are you upset with me inside? Hope in God and give Him who is the health of my countenance, and my God all the praise.

Proverbs 14:32

> The wicked person is driven away in his wickedness: but the righteous ones will have hope in both his physical death and the spiritual (second death).

Plan on examining yourself and partake in the Lord's Supper in remembrance of Christ.

1 Corinthians 11:28

> But let a man examine himself first, and then eat of that bread and drink of that cup!

I take this to mean if I have something warring in my spirit against a brother, or my conscience will not allow me to participate in the memorial service justifiably, it is better to pass on the Lord's Supper. After my heart is right with God then I should participate.

Luke 22:20

After the supper, Jesus told the disciples that this cup is the New Testament "in my blood, which is shed for you."

How often must we participate in the memorial to Christ? I would say consistently and steadfastly, just as the apostles did, and as often as we do participate it should be as the examples were given.

The Scriptures make clear that the disciples were very consistent, not only in the memorial service to the Lord but in study, fellowship, and prayer according to **Acts 2:42.**

> And they continued steadfastly in the apostles' doctrine and fellowship, and in breaking of bread, and in prayers.

Plan on overcoming all obstacles that people and Satan may throw at you.

Revelation 21:6-8

> And Jesus said unto me, it is done. I am alpha and omega, the beginning and the end. I will give unto him that is athirst of the fountain of the water of life freely. He that overcomes shall inherit all things and I will be his God, and he shall be my son. But the fearful, and unbelieving, and the abominable, and murderers, and whoremongers, and sorcerers, and idolaters, and all liars, shall have their part in the lake which burns with fire and brimstone, which is the second death.

Revelation 2:10-11

> Fear none of those things which you shall suffer; behold, Satan will cast some of you into prison, that ye may be tried, and ye will have tribulation for ten days, but be thou faithful unto death, and I will give thee a crown of life. He that hath an ear let him

> hear what the spirit says unto the churches; he that
> overcomes shall not be hurt of the second death.

Plan to choose truth over error in your life.

The spirits of truth and error! Simply put, they are 1) "The spirits of believers that Jesus is the Son of God" and 2) "spirits of antichrist" (1 John 4:3-6).

1 John 4:6

> We are of God: he that knows God hears us; he that
> is not of God doesn't hear us. Hereby we know the
> spirit of truth and the spirit of error.

There are only two types of spirits in the world: truth and error! Compare them to right and wrong! Good and bad! Kind and evil! Straight and narrow! Heaven and hell! It all makes sense when we look at the big picture.

Plan to not let the hard things in life get us down because we don't understand it all.

2 Peter 3:16

Some people create their own destruction because they are unlearned, and wrestle with the hard things to understand in the Bible. There are a lot of things I don't address in the Bible, for the reason I have not studied it in detail enough to comment on it. It is important that I don't struggle with some of the hard things in the Bible, just as this scripture says. If I study like I am instructed to do, and understand the simple plan of salvation, I will not create destruction for myself.

Plan to always resist the devil, knowing that he will flee from you.

James 4:7

If you will resist the devil, he will run away from you. So remember: if you choose to resist the terrorism and violence, its impact on your life vanishes because the fear will not be there once you acquire a working relationship with your Creator.

Plan on being changed from a corruptible to an incorruptible being.

When Jesus returns the next time, all the Christians who have died will rise incorruptible, and then those of us Christians who are alive at that time will be caught up together with them in the clouds to meet the Lord in the air. Then we shall be with Him forever. We all will be changed from a corruptible being into an incorruptible, immortal being just as fast as a blink of the eye!

1 Thessalonians 4:16-17; 1 Corinthians 15:52-54

> If we serve the Lord Jesus Christ, we will receive a reward of the inheritance in the Kingdom of Almighty God. We will share in His Glory there!

Colossians 3:24-25

> Physical death as we know it now will be the last enemy that shall be destroyed.

1 Corinthians 15:26:

[26] The last enemy that shall be destroyed is death.

Plan on being able to accomplish all things in this life.

Philippians 4:13

> I can do all things through Christ which strengthens me.

Plan on abhorring all things in this world that are evil.

Romans 12:9-21

> I am instructed to abhor that which is evil.

Plan on God fashioning your heart as you plan your life.

Psalm 33:13 – 15

> The Lord looks from Heaven and He sees all His creation. In His dwelling place He can look on all the inhabitants of the Earth and He fashions their hearts individually, He considers all their works.

CHAPTER 12

THE ONE THING THAT BOTH ACCUSES ME AND DEFENDS ME

The accusing conscience:

1 Samuel 24:5

When David was in the wilderness of En-ge'di confronted by Saul (his master/the Lord's Anointed) he (David) rose up and cut off the skirt of Saul's robe out of anger. The King James Bible says, "David's heart smote him." Then he told his men to not revolt against the 3,000 men Saul had sent to attack David. David apologized and repented.

Afterward, David was conscience-stricken for having cut off a corner of his robe.

The redeeming conscience:

1 Samuel 25:31 (paraphrased)

When Abigail planned to meet David's soldiers with gifts, she bowed before David (verses 22 and 23) and pleaded that all her evil husband's iniquity (Nabal) be on her shoulders, convincing David that "the Lord will not have on His conscience the staggering burden of needless bloodshed or of having avenged Himself. And when the Lord your God has brought my lord success, remember your servant." David blessed her advice! Her actions caused David to cease avenging himself with his own hands. David told her that none of her husband's men would have been left standing if it weren't for her actions to affect David's conscience (verses 34, 35 and 39). Her husband died, and she became the wife of David, along with one of her five damsels, A-hin'oam of Jez're-el.

When my conscience convicts me of wrongdoing:

2 Samuel 24:10

The power of the conscience in confession: When God's anger was kindled against Israel again, David was moved to take a census of both Israel (800,000) and Judah (500,000). Joab and the captains tried to discourage David from doing this, but they went anyway, for 9 months and 29 days.

Verse 10

David was conscience-stricken after he had counted the fighting men, and he said to the Lord, "I have sinned greatly in what I have done. Now, Lord, I beg you; take away the guilt of your servant. I have done a very foolish thing."

Gad, David's prophet told David that God would require him to bear one of three things because of his sin against God:

1. Bear seven years of famine,
2. Flee from his enemies for three months while they chased him, or
3. Endure three days of pestilence in the land.

David chose the pestilence that killed 70,000 men.

Not listening to your conscience bears consequences:

1 Timothy 1:8-13 (Paul encouraging Timothy to hold on to faith and a good conscience)

> [8]But we know that the law is good, if a man uses it lawfully; [9]knowing this, that the law is not made for a righteous man, but for the lawless and disobedient, for the ungodly and for sinners, for unholy and profane, for murderers of fathers and murderers of mothers, for manslayers, [10]for whoremongers, for them that defile themselves with mankind, for men stealers, for liars, for perjured persons, and if there be any other think that is contrary to sound doctrine, [11]according to the glorious Gospel of the Blessed God, which was committed to my trust. [12]And I thank Christ Jesus our Lord, who hath enabled me for that He counted me faithful, putting me into the ministry; [13]who was before a blasphemer, and a persecutor, and injurious; but I obtained mercy, because I did it ignorantly in unbelief.

The Apostle Paul being confronted by the Lord and being blinded definitely affected his conscience for persecuting the church!

The accusing and defending conscience:

Romans 2:15 (Paul's letter telling that the Gentiles, though not under the Law of Moses, by naturally doing the things contained in the law are in fact a law unto themselves; a law written in their hearts, "bearing witness through their conscience.")

> They show that the requirements of the law are written on their hearts, their consciences also bearing witness, and their thoughts sometimes accusing them and at other times even defending them.

Romans 9:1

> I speak the truth in Christ—I am not lying; my conscience confirms it through the Holy Spirit. *[Paul's anguish over Israel]*

Job 1 (a must-read)

> [20]Then Job arose, and rent his mantle, and shaved his head, and fell down upon the ground, and worshipped, [21]and said, Naked came I out of my mother's womb, and naked shall I return thither: The Lord gave, and the Lord hath taken away; blessed be the name of the Lord. [22]In all this Job sinned not, nor charged God foolishly.

Job 27:6

> I will maintain my innocence and never let go of it; my conscience will not reproach me if I live.

Acts 23:1

> Paul looked straight at the Sanhedrin and said, "My brothers, I have fulfilled my duty to God in all good conscience to this day."

Acts 24:16

> So, I strive always to keep my conscience clear before God and man.

Genesis 20:5

Abraham told King A-bim'e-lech about his wife Sarah, that she was his sister. Sarah also told the king that Abraham was her brother, because they thought there was no godly fear in that place and that Abraham would be killed. Sarah was Abraham's sister by a different mother (Genesis 20:12). Abraham and Sarah agreed that to preserve Abraham's life (Genesis 12:11-13), they agreed (with a good conscience) to call each other brother and sister. The Lord had already plagued the Egyptian Pharaoh because of the same situation (Genesis 12:17).

Genesis 20:5

> Did he not say to me, "She is my sister," and didn't she also say, "He is my brother"? I have done this with a clear conscience and clean hands.

By Abraham's prayers, God healed A-bim'e-lech, his wife, and maidservants so they could have children.

God knows when I am guilty or when I am ignorant of my wrongdoings:

Genesis 20:6

> Then God said to him (Abimilech) in the dream, "Yes, I know you did this with a clear conscience, and so I have kept you from sinning against me. That is why I did not let you touch her."

God is long-suffering, but not forever suffering:

God will allow you to make choices in life, but He will not be mocked, and will turn you over to evil desire if you keep on going against His will.

Examples: homosexuality/sodomy/worship of other gods

Romans 1:27-29

> [27]And likewise also the men, leaving the natural use of the woman, burned in their lust one toward another; men with men working that which is unseemly, and receiving in themselves that recompense of their error which was meet.

> [28]And even **as they did not like to retain God in their knowledge, God gave them over to a reprobate mind, to do those things which are not convenient.**

> [29]Being filled with all unrighteousness, fornication, wickedness, covetousness, maliciousness; full of envy, murder, debate, deceit, malignity; whisperers.

Romans 1:26

> [26]Because of this, **God gave them over to shameful lusts.** Even their women exchanged natural sexual relations for unnatural ones.

Deuteronomy 23:17

> [17]There shall be no whore of the daughters of Israel, nor a sodomite of the sons of Israel.

1 Kings 14:24

> [24]And there were also sodomites in the land: and they did according to all the abominations of the nations which the Lord cast out before the children of Israel.

Acts 7:42

> But **God turned away from them and gave them over** to the worship of the sun, moon and stars.

This agrees with what is written in the book of the prophets: "Did you bring me sacrifices and offerings forty years in the wilderness, people of Israel?"

Is my conscience fulfilling its duty of conviction?

Am I living in the light or in darkness? Am I living in truth or error?

Luke 11:33-36

> [33]No one after lighting a lamp puts it in a cellar or crypt or under a bushel measure, but on a lampstand, that those who are coming in may see the light.

> [34]Your eye is the lamp of your body; when your eye (your conscience) is sound and fulfilling its office, your whole body is full of light; but when it is not sound and is not fulfilling its office, your body is full of darkness.

> [35]Be careful, therefore, that the light that is in you is not darkness.

³⁶If then your entire body is illuminated, having no part dark, it will be wholly bright [with light], as when a lamp with its bright rays gives you light.

1 John 4:5-7

⁵They are from the world and therefore speak from the viewpoint of the world, and the world listens to them. ⁶We are from God, and whoever knows God listens to us; but whoever is not from God does not listen to us. This is how we recognize the spirit of truth and the spirit of falsehood.

Is my conscience allowing me to share in the inheritance of Heaven?

Colossians 1:7-12

⁷You learned it from Epaphras, our dear fellow servant, who is a faithful minister of Christ on our behalf, ⁸and who also told us of your love in the Spirit. ⁹For this reason, since the day we heard about you, we have not stopped praying for you. We continually ask God to fill you with the knowledge of His will through all the wisdom and understanding that the Spirit gives, ¹⁰so that you may live a life worthy of the Lord and please Him in every way: bearing fruit in every good work, growing in the knowledge of God, ¹¹being strengthened with all power according to His glorious might so that you may have great endurance and patience, ¹²and giving joyful thanks to the Father, who has qualified you to share in the inheritance of His holy people in the Kingdom of Light.

If you still wonder how important your conscience is to God, check out these other scriptures when you have time:

1 Timothy 4:2

> Such teachings come through hypocritical liars, whose consciences have been seared as with a hot iron.

2 Timothy 1:3

Thanksgiving

> I thank God, whom I serve, as my ancestors did, with a clear conscience, as night and day I constantly remember you in my prayers.

Titus 1:15

> To the pure, all things are pure, but to those who are corrupted and do not believe, nothing is pure. In fact, both their minds and consciences are corrupted.

Hebrews 9:9

> This is an illustration for the present time, indicating that the gifts and sacrifices being offered were not able to clear the conscience of the worshiper.

Hebrews 9:14

> How much more, then, will the blood of Christ, who through the eternal Spirit offered Himself unblemished to God, cleanse our consciences from

acts that lead to death, so that we may serve the living God!

Hebrews 10:22

Let us draw near to God with a sincere heart and with the full assurance that faith brings, having our hearts sprinkled to cleanse us from a guilty conscience and having our bodies washed with pure water.

Hebrews 13:18

Pray for us. We are sure that we have a clear conscience and desire to live honorably in every way.

1 Peter 3:16

Keeping a clear conscience, so that those who speak maliciously against your good behavior in Christ may be ashamed of their slander.

Conscience-cleansing baptism:

1 Peter 3:21

And this water symbolizes baptism that now saves you also—not the removal of dirt from the body but the pledge of a clear conscience toward God. It saves you by the resurrection of Jesus Christ.

Acts 24:16

So, I strive always to keep my conscience clear before God and man.

Romans 2:15

> They show that the requirements of the law are written on their hearts, **their consciences also bearing witness, and their thoughts sometimes accusing them and at other times even defending them.**

Romans 9:1

Paul's anguish over Israel:

> I speak the truth in Christ—I am not lying; my conscience confirms it through the Holy Spirit.

Romans 13:5

> Therefore, it is necessary to submit to the authorities, not only because of possible punishment but also as a matter of conscience.

1 Corinthians 4:4

> My conscience is clear, but that does not make me innocent. It is the Lord who judges me.

1 Corinthians 8:7

Those who have weak consciences can be defiled with lack of knowledge of the New Testament teachings.

> But not everyone possesses this knowledge. Some people are still so accustomed to idols that when they eat sacrificial food they think of it as having been sacrificed to a god, and since their conscience is weak, it is defiled.

1 Corinthians 8:10

> For if someone with a weak conscience sees you, with all your knowledge, eating in an idol's temple, won't that person be emboldened to eat what is sacrificed to idols?

I as a Christian can wound others who may have weak consciences, thus sinning myself!

1 Corinthians 8:12

> When you sin against them in this way and wound their weak conscience, you sin against Christ.

1 Corinthians 10:25

> Eat anything sold in the meat market without raising questions of conscience.

1 Corinthians 10:27

> If an unbeliever invites you to a meal and you want to go, eat whatever is put before you without raising questions of conscience.

1 Corinthians 10:28

> But if someone says to you, "This has been offered in sacrifice," then do not eat it, both for the sake of the one who told you and for the sake of conscience.

All things are lawful, but not all things are expedient for me as a Christian! My freedom can be judged by another person's conscience. I must be considerate of others' consciences.

1 Corinthians 10:29

> I am referring to the other person's conscience, not yours. For why is my freedom being judged by another's conscience?

2 Corinthians 1:12

Paul's change of plans:

> Now this is our boast: Our conscience testifies that we have conducted ourselves in the world, and especially in our relations with you, with integrity[a] and godly sincerity. We have done so, relying not on worldly wisdom but on God's grace.

The healing power of telling the truth of our shameful ways:

2 Corinthians 4:2

> Rather, we have renounced secret and shameful ways; we do not use deception, nor do we distort the Word of God. On the contrary, by setting forth the truth plainly we commend ourselves to everyone's conscience in the sight of God.

2 Corinthians 5:11

The power of persuasion regarding others' consciences.

The Ministry of Reconciliation:

> Since, then, we know what it is to fear the Lord, we try to persuade others. What we are is plain to God, and I hope it is also plain to your conscience.

1 Timothy 1:5

> The goal of this command is love, which comes from a pure heart and a good conscience and a sincere faith.

1 Timothy 1:19

> Holding on to faith and a good conscience, which some have rejected and so have suffered shipwreck regarding the faith.

1 Timothy 3:9

> They must keep hold of the deep truths of the faith with a clear conscience.

John 8:32

> Then you will know the truth, and the truth will set you free.

Working together to understand how belief and baptism tie together:

2 Peter 1:3

> His divine power has given us everything we need for life and godliness through our knowledge of Him who called us by His own glory and goodness. *[making one's calling and election sure]*

2 Peter 1:10

> Therefore, my brothers, be more eager to make your calling and election sure. For if you do these things, you will never fall.

Revelation 22:19

> And if anyone takes words away from this book of prophecy, God will take away from him his share in the Tree of Life and in the Holy City, which are described in this book.

Is there scriptural justification for me to say that belief is a requirement to fulfill all righteousness and attain salvation?

James 2:18

> But someone will say, "You have faith; I have deeds." Show me your faith without deeds, and I will show you my faith by what I do.

John 11:25

> Jesus said to her, "I am the resurrection and the life. He who believes in me will live, even though he dies."

John 11:26

> And whoever lives and believes in me will never die. Do you believe this?

John 12:44

> Then Jesus cried out, "When a man believes in me, he does not believe in me only, but in the one who sent me.

John 12:46

> I have come into the world as a light, so that no one who believes in me should stay in darkness.

Acts 10:43

> All the prophets testify about Him that everyone who believes in Him receives forgiveness of sins through His name.

Acts 13:39

> Through Him everyone who believes is justified from everything you could not be justified from by the Law of Moses.

Is there scriptural justification for me to say we must have a common understanding on issues that are hard for me to understand?

Absolutely! Because none of us want to create our own destruction! Nor do we want to see our brothers and sisters lost because we simply do not understand biblical instructions.

2 Peter 3:16

He writes the same way in all his letters, speaking in them of these matters. His letters contain some things that are hard to understand, which ignorant and unstable people distort, as they do the other scriptures, to their own destruction.

Is there justification for me to say that the act of (deed) baptism (immersion) is proper for all New Testament Christians?

Absolutely! Jesus Himself said this. "I will show you my faith by what I do" (James 2:18). An action to be taken!

The Baptism of Jesus

Matthew 3:13-17; Mark 1:9-11; Luke 3:21, 22; John 1:31-34

> [13]Then Jesus came from Galilee to the Jordan to be baptized by John. [14]But John tried to deter Him, saying, "I need to be baptized by you, and do you come to me?" [15]Jesus replied, "Let it be so now; it is proper for us to do this to fulfill all righteousness." Then John consented. [16]As soon as Jesus was baptized, He went up out of the water. At that moment Heaven was opened, and He saw the Spirit of God descending like a dove and lighting on Him. [17]And a voice from Heaven said, "This is my Son, whom I love; with Him I am well pleased."

Matthew 3:15

> Jesus replied, "Let it be so now; it is proper for us to do this to fulfill all righteousness." Then John consented.

Matthew 3:16

> As soon as Jesus was baptized, He went up out of the water. At that moment Heaven was opened, and

Steve C. Varner

He saw the Spirit of God descending like a dove and lighting on Him.

Romans 10:4

Christ is the end of the law so that there may be righteousness for everyone who believes.

Is there justification for me to say that baptism (immersion in water) is a necessity for all New Testament Christians to be saved?

Absolutely! The apostles said this.

1 Peter 3:17-21

[17]It is better, if it is God's will, to suffer for doing good than for doing evil. [18]For Christ died for sins once for all, the righteous for the unrighteous, to bring you to God. He was put to death in the body but made alive by the Spirit, [19]through whom also He went and preached to the spirits in prison [20]who disobeyed long ago when God waited patiently in the days of Noah while the ark was being built. In it only a few people, eight in all, were saved through water, [21]and **this water symbolizes baptism that now saves you also—not the removal of dirt from the body but the pledge of a good conscience toward God. It saves you by the resurrection of Jesus Christ, [22]who has gone into Heaven and is at God's right hand—with angels, authorities and powers in submission to Him.**

Is there justification for me to say that baptism (immersion in water) and belief go hand in hand and must be an (all-inclusive)

action for New Testament Christians to be saved; otherwise we will be subjected to condemnation?

Absolutely!

Mark 16:16

> Whoever believes and is baptized will be saved, but whoever does not believe will be condemned.

John 3:15

> That everyone who believes in Him may have eternal life.

John 3:16

> For God so loved the world that He gave His one and only Son, that whoever believes in Him shall not perish but have eternal life.

John 3:18

> Whoever believes in Him is not condemned, but whoever does not believe stands condemned already because he has not believed in the name of God's one and only Son.

Is there justification for me to say that without baptism (immersion in water) and belief, I stand rejected and will not see life because God's wrath remains on me?

Absolutely!

John 3:36

> Whoever believes in the Son has eternal life, but whoever rejects the Son will not see life, for God's wrath remains on him.

John 3:16

> For God so loved the world that He gave His one and only Son, that whoever believes in Him shall not perish but have eternal life.

Is there justification for me to say that without baptism (immersion in water) and belief, I have not crossed over from death unto life everlasting?

Absolutely!

John 5:24

> I tell you the truth, whoever hears my Word and believes Him who sent me has eternal life and will not be condemned; he has crossed over from death to life.

John 6:40

> For my Father's will is that everyone who looks to the Son and believes in Him shall have eternal life, and I will raise him up at the last day.

John 6:35

> Then Jesus declared, "I am the bread of life. He who comes to me will never go hungry, and he who believes in me will never be thirsty."

Is there justification for me to say that without baptism and receiving the gift of the Holy Spirit, I cannot enter the Kingdom of God?

Absolutely! Jesus Himself said this.

John 3:5

> Jesus answered, "I tell you the truth, no one can enter the Kingdom of God unless he is born of water and the Spirit."

Acts 8:36

> As they traveled along the road, they came to some water and the eunuch said, "Look, here is water. Why shouldn't I be baptized?"

Mark 16:16

> Whoever believes and is baptized will be saved, but whoever does not believe will be condemned.

Romans 9:1

> I speak the truth in Christ—I am not lying; my conscience confirms it in the Holy Spirit. *[God's sovereign choice]*

Is there justification for me to say that without baptism and receiving the gift of the Holy Spirit, I cannot put on the character of Christ?

Absolutely!

Steve C. Varner

Galatians 3:27

> For all of you who were baptized into Christ have
> clothed yourselves with Christ.

**Is there justification for me to say that without baptism, I cannot
live with a clear conscience toward God?**

Absolutely!

1 Peter 3:21

> And this water symbolizes baptism that now saves
> you also—not the removal of dirt from the body but
> the pledge of a good conscience toward God. It saves
> you by the resurrection of Jesus Christ.

**Is there justification for me to say that I (as a Christian) should
never deny anyone to be baptized if requested?**

Absolutely!

Acts 8:36

> As they traveled along the road, they came to some
> water and the eunuch said, "Look, here is water.
> Why shouldn't I be baptized?"

Acts 8:38

> And he gave orders to stop the chariot. Then both
> Philip and the eunuch went down into the water and
> Philip baptized him.

Is there justification for me to say that New Testament Christians can only receive remission of sin and the gift of the Comforter (the Holy Spirit) after baptism? And that we have been warned and pleaded with to complete this command before we are added to the Body of Christ?

Matthew 3:16

> As soon as Jesus was baptized, He went up out of the water. At that moment Heaven was opened, and He saw the Spirit of God descending like a dove and lighting on Him.

Acts 2:34-41

> [34]For David did not ascend to Heaven, and yet he said, "The Lord said to my lord: 'Sit at my right hand [35]until I make your enemies a footstool for your feet." [36]Therefore let all Israel be assured of this: God has made this Jesus, whom you crucified, both Lord and Christ." **[37]When the people heard this, they were cut to the heart and said to Peter and the other apostles, "Brothers, what shall we do?" [38] Peter replied, "Repent and be baptized, every one of you, in the name of Jesus Christ for the forgiveness of your sins. And you will receive the gift of the Holy Spirit. [39]The promise is for you and your children and for all who are far off—for all whom the Lord our God will call." [40]With many other words he warned them; and he pleaded with them, "Save yourselves from this corrupt generation." [41]Those who accepted his message were baptized, and about three thousand were added to their number that day.**

Is there justification for me to say that those of us who accept baptism, the remission of our sin, and the gift of the Holy Spirit are spiritually reborn and given different gifts according to God's will? And that these acts of obedience save us, not because of what we have done, but solely because of God's mercy on us?

Absolutely!

Titus 3:5

> He saved us, not because of righteous things we had done, but because of His mercy. He saved us through the washing of rebirth and renewal by the Holy Spirit.

John 6:40

> For my Father's will is that everyone who looks to the Son and believes in Him shall have eternal life, and I will raise him up at the last day.

John 6:47

> I tell you the truth, he who believes has everlasting life.

John 7:38

> Whoever believes in me, as the Scripture has said, streams of living water will flow from within him.

Is there justification for me to deny that some of God's chosen men received the Holy Spirit just by the laying on hands, even though I am instructed to show my commitment to the cause of Christ by cleansing my conscience in this manner?

Absolutely not!

Acts 19:6 NIV

> When Paul placed his hands on them, the Holy Spirit came on them, and they spoke in tongues and prophesied.

Is there justification for me to say that we all have been warned, and that we should not put this act of obedience off any longer? That in so doing, we test and try Almighty God in His judgment, which it does, in fact make God angry, and that we will not enter God's rest if we neglect His commandments?

Absolutely!

Hebrews 3

Jesus greater than Moses

> Therefore, holy brothers and sisters, who share in the heavenly calling, fix your thoughts on Jesus, whom we acknowledge as our apostle and high priest. [2]He was faithful to the one who appointed Him, just as Moses was faithful in all God's house. [3]Jesus has been found worthy of greater honor than Moses, just as the builder of a house has greater honor than the house itself. [4]For every house is built by someone, but God is the builder of everything. [5]Moses was faithful as a servant in all God's house, bearing witness to what would be spoken by God in the future. [6]But Christ is faithful as the Son over God's house. And we are His house, if indeed we hold firmly to our confidence and the hope in which we glory. [7]So, as the Holy Spirit says: Today, if you

hear His voice, [8]do not harden your hearts as you did in the rebellion, during the time of testing in the wilderness, [9]where your ancestors tested and tried me, though for forty years they saw what I did. [10]That is why I was angry with that generation; I said, 'Their hearts are always going astray, and they have not known my ways. [11]So I declared an oath an my anger, they shall never enter my rest. [12]See to it, brothers and sisters, that none of you has a sinful, unbelieving heart that turns away from the living God. [13]But encourage one another daily, if it is called "Today," so that none of you may be hardened by sin's deceitfulness. [14]We have come to share in Christ, if indeed we hold our original conviction firmly to the very end. [15]As has just been said: [16]Who were they who heard and rebelled? Were they not all those Moses led out of Egypt? [17]And with whom was He angry for forty years? Was it not with those who sinned, whose bodies perished in the wilderness? [18]And to whom did God swear that they would never enter His rest if not to those who disobeyed? [19]So we see that they were not able to enter, because of their unbelief.

Is there justification for me to say that we can only purify ourselves by obeying the truth of God's Word?

Absolutely!

1 Peter 1:22-23

[22]Now that you have purified yourselves by obeying the truth so that you have sincere love for each other, love one another deeply, from the heart. [23]For you have been born again, not of perishable seed, but

of imperishable, through the living and enduring
Word of God.

**Is there justification for me to say that Jesus is my example, He is
the one who set the standard for us to clean our conscience and
fulfill all righteousness through baptism?**

Absolutely!

Matthew 3:15

> Jesus replied, "Let it be so now; it is proper for us to
> do this to fulfill all righteousness."

I concluded that even though this is one of the hardest things for
me to understand, I can no more separate belief and baptism from
God's plan of salvation than I could hearing, repentance, confession,
obedience, prayer, partaking of the Lord's Supper, fellowship, worship,
singing psalms and hymns and spiritual songs, admonishing and
exhorting one another, study of God's Word and not following the
traditions of men, as we are warned not to do. By applying all of
God's Holy Word together we make our calling and election sure!

Just as **2 Peter 1:3** NIV says:

> His divine power has given us everything we need
> for life and godliness through our knowledge of
> Him who called us by His own glory and goodness!

**The last questions I must ask myself: am I guilty of setting aside
the Commandments of God to observe the traditions of my family
or my own?**

Mark 7:8

You have let go of the commands of God and are holding on to human traditions.

Mark 7:9

You have a fine way of setting aside the commands of God to observe your own traditions.

CHAPTER 13

OUR REASONABLE SERVICE

To those who do not believe that Jesus is the Son of God, that He was born of the Virgin Mary (He came in the flesh), that He died (went into Sheol and preached to the lost souls) for the sin of the world and rose on the third day, and ascended back to Heaven to sit at the right hand of the Creator (the Father), and that He sent the Holy Spirit to those of us who are His true disciples, Satan does two things:

Satan blinds (creates a veil) the minds of those who do not believe, and he prevents the light of the Gospel of Christ (the image of God) from shining on those who do not believe.

The deception Satan brings to this Earth is and will always be under the scrutiny of the Body of Christ!

To be on guard for the things that Satan tempts us with, in his deception, we must learn to resist him, knowing that he is a coward:

James 4:7

> Submit yourselves, then, to God. Resist the devil,
> and he will flee from you.

The only way these blinded souls can break out of Satan's bondage is by us, as Christians, preaching the knowledge of God's glory as we see it in the face of the Lord Jesus:

John 16:7-11

> [7]But very truly I tell you, it is for your good that I am going away. Unless I go away, the Advocate will not come to you; but if I go, I will send Him to you. [8]When He comes, He will prove the world to be in the wrong about sin and righteousness and judgment: [9]about sin, because people do not believe in me; [10]about righteousness, because I am going to the Father, where you can see me no longer; [11]and about judgment, because the prince of this world now stands condemned.

The spiritually dead are those who are carnally minded instead of spiritually minded:

Romans 8:6

> For to be carnally minded is death; but to be spiritually minded is life and peace.

Romans 8:7

> Because the carnal mind is enmity against God: for it is not subject to the law of God, neither indeed can be.

Romans 6:11

> Likewise reckon ye also yourselves to be dead indeed unto sin, but alive unto God through Jesus Christ our Lord.

I inherited a carnal mind through the sins of Adam and Eve, but in Christ I inherit life eternal and become a new spiritual-minded person. This is called "being made alive" or a "rebirth."

1 Corinthians 15:22

> For as in Adam all die, even so in Christ shall all be made alive.

Jesus Christ (the Word) became flesh and left the glory of Heaven to bring salvation unto all men in the form of a man; once He fulfilled His mission, He returned into His original glory at the right hand of Almighty God and then He sent the Comforter (the Holy Spirit) to guide us as we live our lives in Him.

When Jesus rose from the grave He promised that He would send another Comforter (other than Himself) to abide with us believers forever. This Comforter is our guide into all righteousness! He reminds us of what Christ told us while He was here on Earth:

John 14:16

> And I will pray the Father, and He shall give you another Comforter, that He may abide with you forever;

John 14:26

> But the Comforter, which is the Holy Ghost, whom the Father will send in my name, He shall teach you all things, and bring all things to your remembrance, whatsoever I have said unto you.

God the Father, God the Son, and God the Comforter (Holy Spirit) are one in the same being, this is called the Godhead Bodily:

Acts 17:29

> Forasmuch then as we are the offspring of God, we ought not to think that the Godhead is like unto gold, or silver, or stone, graven by art and man's device.

Romans 1:20

> For the invisible things of Him from the creation of the world are clearly seen, being understood by the things that are made, even His eternal power and Godhead; so that they are without excuse.

Colossians 2:9

> For in Him (Jesus) dwelleth all the fullness of the Godhead Bodily.

Who could keep our Savior from returning to His original glory after such exceeding wonderful kindness to redeem us back to His Father? This was His mission, to give His life for us (become the propitiation for our sins) and return to His original glory!

Luke 24:26

> Ought not Christ to have suffered these things, and to enter His glory?

Romans 3:25

> Whom God hath set forth to be a propitiation (sacrifice) through faith in His blood, to declare His righteousness for the remission of sins that are past, through the forbearance of God.

1 John 2:2

> And He is the propitiation (sacrifice) for our sins: and not for ours only, but also for the sins of the whole world.

It is our duty as Christians to obey the Great Commission given by Jesus Himself in Mark 16:

> [15]He said to them, "Go into all the world and preach the Gospel to all creation. [16]Whoever believes and is baptized will be saved, but whoever does not believe will be condemned."

Why should we remind our brothers and sisters in Christ and encourage, admonish and exhort each other, no matter how unworthy we are? Why would God use such people as me (a sinner), as the Apostle Paul (a murderer), as the woman at the well (an adulteress), to bring our loved ones into remembrance of the ways of Christ?

1 Corinthians 4:17

> For this cause have I sent unto you Timotheus, who is my beloved son, and faithful in the Lord, who shall bring you into remembrance of my ways which be in Christ, as I teach everywhere in every church.

2 Corinthians 10:5

> Casting down imaginations, and every high thing that exalteth itself against the knowledge of God and bringing into captivity every thought to the obedience of Christ.

Steve C. Varner

Perhaps our reasonable service is not only to help others, but to help ourselves discern who is of God and who is of Satan, "the great deceiver:"

2 Corinthians 11:13

> For such are false apostles, deceitful workers, transforming themselves into the apostles of Christ.

Matthew 7:15

> Beware of false prophets, which come to you in sheep's clothing, but inwardly they are ravening wolves.

Matthew 24:11

> And many false prophets shall rise and shall deceive many.

Matthew 24:24

> For there shall arise false Christs, and false prophets, and shall shew great signs and wonders; insomuch that, if it were possible, they shall deceive the very elect.

Mark 13:22

> For false Christs and false prophets shall rise, and shall shew signs and wonders, to seduce, if it were possible, even the elect.

Luke 6:26

> Woe unto you, when all men shall speak well of you!
> For so did their fathers to the false prophets.

2 Peter 2:1

> But there were false prophets also among the people,
> even as there shall be false teachers among you,
> who privily shall bring in damnable heresies, even
> denying the Lord that bought them, and bring upon
> themselves swift destruction.

1 John 4:1

> Beloved, believe not every spirit, but try the spirits
> whether they are of God: because many false
> prophets are gone out into the world.

A warning against denying that Jesus came in the flesh:

1 John 2:18

> Dear children, this is the last hour; and as you have
> heard that the antichrist is coming, even now many
> antichrists have come. This is how we know it is the
> last hour.

2 John 1:7

> I say this because many deceivers, who do not
> acknowledge Jesus Christ as coming in the flesh,
> have gone out into the world. Any such person is the
> deceiver and the antichrist.

This is our reasonable service, to become ministers of the Gospel and renounce our past ways, tell the truth and become servants to all who are blinded! Those who are not blinded by Satan's veil have the knowledge needed to also fulfill their calling. The choice to serve is ours. If we choose not to acknowledge Christ and who He claims to be, we then are classified as antichrist. And there are many!

Romans 12:1

> I beseech you therefore, brethren, by the mercies of God, that ye present your bodies a living sacrifice, holy, acceptable unto God, which is your reasonable service.

Luke 9:62

> Jesus replied, "No one who puts a hand to the plow and looks back is fit for service in the Kingdom of God."

Luke 12:34-40

> [34]For where your treasure is, there your heart will be also. [35]"Be dressed ready for service and keep your lamps burning, [36]like servants waiting for their master to return from a wedding banquet, so that when he comes and knocks they can immediately open the door for him. [37]It will be good for those servants whose master finds them watching when he comes. Truly I tell you, he will dress himself to serve, will have them recline at the table and will come and wait on them. [38]It will be good for those servants whose master finds them ready, even if he comes in the middle of the night or toward daybreak. [39]But understand this: If the owner of the house had known at what hour the thief was coming, he would not have let his house be broken into. [40]You also

must be ready, because the Son of Man will come at an hour when you do not expect Him."

Romans 12:3

For by the grace given me I say to every one of you: Do not think of yourself more highly than you ought, but rather think of yourself with sober judgment, in accordance with the faith God has distributed to each of you. *[humble service in the Body of Christ]*

Romans 15:17

Therefore, I glory in Christ Jesus in my service to God.

1 Corinthians 3:9

For we are co-workers in God's service; you are God's field, God's building.

1 Corinthians 12:5

There are different kinds of service, but the same Lord.

My reasonable service is to teach anyone and everyone that there is verification by Scripture that God the Father, the Son and the Holy Spirit are one, and that the Bible is the only authorized plan of salvation!

2 Timothy 3:15-17; 1 Thessalonians 2:13; 2 Peter 1:21

The Bible to is the only inspired, infallible and authoritative Word of God.

CHAPTER 14

THE GODHEAD BODILY

There is one true God eternally existent in three persons: The Father, Son and Holy Spirit (Deuteronomy 6:4; Isaiah 43:10-11; Matthew 28:18-20; Luke 3:22). In the beginning was the Word (Jesus was the Word, the Word was God and the Word Became Flesh: John 1:1; John 1:14). The Godhead Bodily includes God, Jesus, the Holy Spirit, and Mankind as the Holy Spirit dwells in all true believers.

In the deity of our Lord Jesus Christ, in His virgin birth, sinless life, miracles, Jesus as the atonement for our sins by His death on the cross, He experienced bodily resurrection, ascension to the Father and that all of mankind will bow before Him in His personal return to power and glory (Matthew 1:23; Luke 1:31-32; Acts 10:37-38; Acts 2:22; Hebrews 7:26-27; 1 Corinthians 15:3-5; 2 Corinthians 5:21-6:1; Matthew 28:6; Luke 24:39; 1 Corinthians 15:4-6; Acts 1:9-11; Philippians 2:9-11; Hebrew 1:3). Belief in this concept is a must (Acts 10:43).

Regeneration by the Holy Spirit is essential for the salvation of sinful man; a person must experience a spiritual rebirth. Only through the power of the Holy Spirit is the Christian able to live a godlier life. Salvation comes when one is born of the water and the Spirit (Acts 2:38; Acts 10:43; Galatians 3:27; Romans 10:12-13; Ephesians 2:8-10; Titus 2:11; Titus 3:4-8; Romans 8:16; Ephesians 4:24; Titus 2:12).

Spiritual Fullness in Christ

If I am truly born of the water and the Spirit, I come into fullness as a part of the Godhead Bodily, Oh, you say! That is blasphemy! Read Colossians 2:9:

> [6]So then, just as you received Christ Jesus as Lord, continue to live your lives in Him, [7]rooted and built up in Him, strengthened in the faith as you were taught, and overflowing with thankfulness.

> [8]See to it that no one takes you captive through hollow and deceptive philosophy, which depends on human tradition and the elemental spiritual forces[a] of this world rather than on Christ.

> **[9]For in Christ all the fullness of the Deity lives in bodily form, [10]and in Christ you have been brought to fullness.** He is the head over every power and authority. [11]In Him you were also circumcised with a circumcision not performed by human hands. **Your whole self, ruled by the flesh was put off when you were circumcised by Christ, [12]having been buried with Him in baptism, in which you were also raised with Him through your faith in the working of God, who raised Him from the dead.**

You and I are the Temple of the Holy Spirit here on Earth, not buildings nor anything made with hands (1 Corinthians 6:19; 1 Corinthians 3:17).

There is a resurrection of both the saved and the lost—the saved to eternal life in Heaven, the lost to hell. Hell is real suffering and is everlasting punishment, because our souls are not annihilated.

(1 Thessalonians 4:15-17; Romans 3:23-24; 1 Corinthians 15:51-52; Revelations 20:11-15; Revelations 21:6-8).

Jesus Christ rose from the dead and is returning soon (Zechariah 14:4-5, Matthew 24:26; Matthew 24:30; Revelations 1:7; Relations 19:11-13).

The Great Commission of the church is to go into the entire world and preach the Gospel to every person, using every modern means of communication available to us. He that believes and is baptized for the remission of sins shall be saved and will receive the gift of the Holy Spirit (Acts 10:43; Galatians 3:27; Acts 2:38; Mark 16:15; Luke 14:23; Matthew 28:19-20; Acts 1:7-8; Mark 16:15-16). We must confess Jesus as our Lord and Savior for Jesus to confess us before the Father in Heaven (Matthew 10:32; Revelations 3:5; Luke 12:8).

Do you believe in the spiritual unity of believers through the working of the Holy Spirit and the Lord Jesus Christ? (Ephesians 4:11-13; Psalm 133:1; Philippians 2:1-3)

Do you believe in holy Christian living, and to have concern for the hurts and social needs of our fellow men? (Colossians 3:12-14; Romans 15:1-2)

We must dedicate ourselves anew to the service of our Lord and to His authority over our lives. (Colossians 2:9-11; Ephesians 6:7-8)

We are not bound by Old Testament law, where remembrance of our sins is required each year (Hebrews 10:2-3). The Law of Grace (New Testament Christianity) superseded the laws of the patriarchs and the Law of Moses which God first implemented (Ephesians 1:7; Galatians 3:24-25).

Obey the teachings that have been handed down through the Apostles, with reverence (1 Corinthians 11:2).

CHAPTER 15

THE HARD THINGS TO UNDERSTAND

2 Peter 3:16

He writes the same way in all his letters, speaking in them of these matters. His letters contain some things that are hard to understand, which ignorant and unstable people distort, as they do the other scriptures, to their own destruction.

We must remember this scripture so that we are not led into destruction!

**

One hard thing for me to understand:

1 Corinthians 1:10

> Now I plead with you, brethren, by the name of our Lord Jesus Christ, that you all speak the same thing, and that there be no divisions among you, but that you be perfectly joined together in the same mind and in the same judgment.

**

Steve C. Varner

A question I often ask myself: how do we as brothers and sisters in Christ reconcile our differences?

1 Corinthians 9:22

> To the weak I became weak, to win the weak. I have become all things to all people so that by all possible means I might save some.

Romans 3:23

> For all have sinned and fall short of the glory of God.

Isaiah 1:18

> "Come now, and let us reason together," says the Lord, "though your sins are like scarlet, they shall be as white as snow; though they are red like crimson, they shall be as wool."

**

How do I fulfill this scripture of "shall be perfect"? Is it just about not wavering in my faith? I will never be perfect while on Earth, so I am still obligated to strive to fulfill the commands I have been given. I must remember, it is not about me! It is about the glory of God!

Matthew 5:48

> **Therefore, you shall be perfect, just as your Father in Heaven is perfect.**

Psalm 18:32

> It is God who arms me with strength and makes my way perfect.

Psalm 119:96

> I have seen the consummation of all perfection, but Your commandment is exceedingly broad.

Matthew 19:21

> Jesus said to him, "If you want to be perfect, go, sell what you have and give to the poor, and you will have treasure in Heaven; and come, follow me."

2 Corinthians 7:1

> Therefore, having these promises, beloved, let us cleanse ourselves from all filthiness of the flesh and spirit, perfecting holiness in the fear of God.

**

Unity of faith should be our goal!

Ephesians 4:13

> Until we all come to the unity of the faith and of the knowledge of the Son of God, to a perfect man, to the measure of the stature of the fullness of Christ.

Philippians 3:12

> Not that I have already attained, or am already
> perfected; but I press on, that I may lay hold of that
> for which Christ Jesus has also laid hold of me.
> *[pressing toward the goal]*

Colossians 1:28 (the Apostle Paul said this)

> Him we preach, warning every man and teaching
> every man in all wisdom, that we may present every
> man perfect in Christ Jesus.

**

Three commands given by Jesus Himself!

Matthew 28:18-20

> [18]Then Jesus came to them and said, "All authority
> in Heaven and on Earth has been given to me.
> [19]Therefore go and make disciples of all nations,
> baptizing them in the name of the Father and of the
> Son and of the Holy Spirit, [20]and teaching them to
> obey everything I have commanded you. And surely,
> I am with you always, to the very end of the age."

James 1:25

> But he who looks into the perfect law of liberty and
> continues in it and is not a forgetful hearer but a
> doer of the work, this one will be blessed in what
> he does.

James 2:22

> Do you see that faith was working together with His
> works, and by works faith was made perfect?

**

The idea of going on unto perfection is a continual process of being
sanctified!

Hebrews 6:1

> Therefore, leaving the discussion of the elementary
> principles of Christ, let us go on to perfection, not
> laying again the foundation of repentance from
> dead works and of faith toward God.

Hebrews 10:14

> For by one offering He (Jesus) has perfected forever
> those who are being sanctified.

Hebrews 12:23

> To the general assembly and church of the firstborn
> who are registered in Heaven, to God the Judge of
> all, to the spirits of just men made perfect.

James 1:4

> But let patience have its perfect work, that you may
> be perfect and complete, lacking nothing.

**

It is all about giving God the glory and expecting the exceeding wonderful gift of being presented to God as white as snow, even though we are dirty!

1 Peter 5:10

> But may the God of all grace, who called us to His eternal glory by Christ Jesus, after you have suffered a while, perfect, establish, strengthen, and settle you.

True discipleship:

1 John 2:5

> But whoever keeps His Word, truly the love of God is perfected in him. By this we know that we are in Him.

1 John 4:12

> No one has seen God at any time. If we love one another, God abides in us, and His love has been perfected in us. *[seeing God through love]*

**

Perfect love has no part with fear, and works are an integral part of obtaining perfection in the sight of God, because faith without works is dead:

1 John 4:18

> There is no fear in love; but perfect love casts out fear, because fear involves torment. But he who fears has not been made perfect in love.

**

A WARNING!

Revelation 3:2

> Be watchful, and strengthen the things which remain, that are ready to die, for I have not found your works perfect before God.

**

A PROMISE!

1 John 2:5

> But whoever keeps His Word, truly the love of God is perfected in him. By this we know that we are in Him.

Revelation 3:5

> He who overcomes shall be clothed in white garments, and I will not blot out his name from the Book of Life; but I will confess his name before my Father and before His angels.

Revelation 3:21

> To him who overcomes I will grant to sit with me on my throne, as I also overcame and sat down with my Father on His throne.

Matthew 10:32

> Therefore, whoever confesses me before men, him I will also confess before my Father who is in Heaven. *[confess Christ before men]*

Romans 8:17

> Now if we are children, then we are heirs—heirs of God and co-heirs with Christ, if indeed we share in His sufferings in order that we may also share in His glory.

Romans 8:21

> That the creation itself will be liberated from its bondage to decay and brought into the freedom and glory of the children of God.

**

Some are blinded so they cannot see the glory of Almighty God in the face of Christ!

2 Corinthians 4:4

> The god (Satan) of this age has blinded the minds of unbelievers, so that they cannot see the light of the Gospel that displays the glory of Christ, who is the image of God.

**

Our duty to share the light:

2 Corinthians 4:6

> For God, who said, "Let light shine out of darkness,"
> made His light shine in our hearts to give us the
> light of the knowledge of God's glory displayed in
> the face of Christ.

**

Our duty in the Great Commission is to reach as many souls for
Christ in this short period of time here on Earth:

2 Corinthians 4:15

> All this is for your benefit, so that the grace that
> is reaching more and more people may cause
> thanksgiving to overflow to the glory of God.

All our needs will be met through the riches of God's glory:

Philippians 4:19

> And my God will meet all your needs according to
> the riches of His glory in Christ Jesus.

Colossians 1:27

> To them God has chosen to make known among the
> Gentiles the glorious riches of this mystery, which is
> Christ in you, the hope of glory.

1 Peter 4:11

> If anyone speaks, they should do so as one who
> speaks the very words of God. If anyone serves, they

should do so with the strength God provides, so that in all things God may be praised through Jesus Christ. To Him be the glory and the power for ever and ever. Amen.

**

What an "exceeding wonderful kindness" we have been given!

CHAPTER 16

THE IRREVOCABLE CALLING

Romans 10:16-21

> [16]But not all the Israelites accepted the good news. For Isaiah says, "Lord, who has believed our message?" [17]Consequently, faith comes from hearing the message, and the message is heard through the Word about Christ. [18]But I ask: Did they not hear? Of course, they did: "Their voice has gone out into all the Earth, their words to the ends of the world."

> [19]Again I ask: Did Israel not understand? First, Moses says, "I will make you envious by those who are not a nation; I will make you angry by a nation that has no understanding."

> [20]And Isaiah boldly says, "I was found by those who did not seek me; I revealed myself to those who did not ask for me." [21]But concerning Israel he says, "All day long I have held out my hands to a disobedient and obstinate people."

The Remnant of Israel

Romans 11

¹I ask then: Did God reject His people? By no means! I am an Israelite myself, a descendant of Abraham, from the tribe of Benjamin. ²God did not reject His people, whom He foreknew. Don't you know what Scripture says in the passage about Elijah—how he appealed to God against Israel: ³"Lord, they have killed your prophets and torn down your altars; I am the only one left, and they are trying to kill me"? ⁴And what was God's answer to him? "I have reserved for myself seven thousand who have not bowed the knee to Baal." ⁵So too, now there is a remnant chosen by grace. ⁶And if by grace, then it cannot be based on works; if it were, grace would no longer be grace.

(See 1 Kings 18:22 where Elijah thought he would be the only remnant.)

⁷What then? What the people of Israel sought so earnestly they did not obtain. The elect among them did, but the others were hardened, ⁸as it is written: "God gave them a spirit of stupor, eyes that could not see and ears that could not hear, to this very day."

⁹And David says: "May their table become a snare and a trap, a stumbling block and a retribution for them. ¹⁰May their eyes be darkened so they cannot see, and their backs be bent forever."

(See also Isaiah 29:9-10)

> [11]Again I ask: Did they stumble to fall beyond recovery? Not at all! Rather, because of their transgression, salvation has come to the Gentiles to make Israel envious."

Note! God Almighty used the transgression of His chosen race to bring salvation to the Gentiles and to make His chosen people envious.

John 10:14-18

> [14]"I am the Good Shepherd; I know my sheep and my sheep know me— [15]just as the Father knows me and I know the Father—and I lay down my life for the sheep. [16]I have other sheep that are not of this sheep pen. I must bring them also. They too will listen to my voice, and there shall be one flock and one shepherd. [17]The reason my Father loves me is that I lay down my life—only to take it up again. [18]No one takes it from me, but I lay it down of my own accord. I have authority to lay it down and authority to take it up again. This command I received from my Father."

I am one of those other sheep! I am a Gentile because I am not a Jew!

Romans Chapter 11

> [12]But if their transgression means riches for the world, and their loss means riches for the Gentiles, how much greater riches will their full inclusion bring!

> [13]I am talking to you Gentiles. Since I am the apostle to the Gentiles, I take pride in my ministry [14]in the hope that I may somehow arouse my own people to envy and save some of them.

Note: Dis-fellowship brings reconciliation:

> [15]For if their rejection brought reconciliation to the world, what will their acceptance be but life from the dead? [16]If the part of the dough offered as first fruits is holy, then the whole batch is holy; if the root is holy, so are the branches.

> [17]If some of the branches have been broken off, and you, though a wild olive shoot, have been grafted in among the others and now share in the nourishing sap from the olive root, [18]do not consider yourself to be superior to those other branches. If you do, consider this: You do not support the root, but the root supports you. [19]You will say then, "Branches were broken off so that I could be grafted in." [20]Granted (true). But they (Israelites) were broken off because of unbelief, and you stand by faith. Do not be arrogant, but tremble. [21]For if God did not spare the natural branches, He will not spare you either.

The irrevocable calling is for the remnant. What about those who repent? Another one of those provisions!

A condition:

> [22]Consider therefore the kindness and sternness of God: *(read Proverbs 15:10)* sternness to those who fell, but kindness to you, if you continue in His kindness. Otherwise, you also will be cut off. [23] And if they do

not persist in unbelief, they will be grafted in, for God is able to graft them in again. ²⁴After all, if you were cut out of an olive tree that is wild by nature, and contrary to nature were grafted into a cultivated olive tree, how much more readily will these, the natural branches, be grafted into their own olive tree! *(the chosen race)*

All Israel will be saved:

²⁵I do not want you to be ignorant of this mystery, brothers and sisters, so that you may not be conceited: Israel has experienced a hardening in part until the full number of the Gentiles has come in, ²⁶and in this way all Israel will be saved. As it is written: *(see Isaiah 59:20. -21)*

"The deliverer will come from Zion; He will turn godlessness away from Jacob. ²⁷And this is[f] my covenant with them when I take away their sins."

²⁸As far as the Gospel is concerned, they are enemies for your sake; but as far as election is concerned, they are loved because of the patriarchs, ²⁹or God's gifts and His call are irrevocable. ³⁰Just as you who were at one time disobedient to God have now received mercy because of their disobedience, ³¹so they too have now become disobedient in order that they too may now receive mercy because of God's mercy to you. ³²For God has bound everyone over to disobedience so that He may have mercy on them all.

God did predestine all of those He foreknew! (Read Romans 8:28-30)

²⁸And we know that in all things God works for the good of those who love Him, who[i] have been

called according to His purpose. [29]For those God foreknew He also predestined to be conformed to the image of His Son, that He might be the firstborn among many brothers and sisters. [30]And those He predestined, He also called; those He called, He also justified; those He justified, He also glorified.

It would be wrong for me to say I don't believe in pre-destination. I would be denying the Holy Scriptures. Does this mean I don't believe in freedom of choice? No! The Israelites who did not repent made their own choice to obey God. The remnant did repent.

Doxology

[33]Oh, the depth of the riches of the wisdom and[i]
knowledge of God!
How unsearchable His judgments,
and His paths beyond tracing out!
[34]"Who has known the mind of the Lord?
Or who has been his Counselor?"
[35]"Who has ever given to God,
that God should repay them?"
[36]For from Him and through Him and for Him are
all things.
To Him be the glory forever! Amen.

CHAPTER 17

THE TIME OF TESTING

For those who still question if Christ is God, you must make a choice to either deny it or believe it as spoken from the words of Jesus Himself. If you still in doubt, read the following scriptures:

John 17:11-23 (Jesus' Prayer)

> [11]I will remain in the world no longer, but they are still in the world, and I am coming to you. Holy Father protect them by the power of your name, the name you gave me, so that they may be one as we are one. [12]While I was with them, I protected them and kept them safe by that name you gave me. None has been lost except the one doomed to destruction so that Scripture would be fulfilled.

> [13]"I am coming to you now, but I say these things while I am still in the world, so that they may have the full measure of my joy within them. [14]I have given them your Word and the world has hated them, for they are not of the world any more than I am of the world.

By this statement, Jesus is confirming that those spiritually minded are no longer carnal, and we are not of this world. We are destined to share in God's glory!

> ¹⁵My prayer is not that you take them out of the world but that you protect them from the evil one. ¹⁶They are not of the world, even as I am not of it. ¹⁷Sanctify them by the truth; your Word is truth. ¹⁸As you sent me into the world, I have sent them into the world. ¹⁹For them I sanctify myself, that they too may be truly sanctified.

Jesus just said that He sent us into the world just like God sent Him here!

Jesus prays for all believers:

> ²⁰"My prayer is not for them alone. I pray also for those who will believe in me through their message, ²¹that all of them may be one, Father, just as you are in me and I am in you. May they also be in us so that the world may believe that you have sent me. ²²I have given them the glory that you gave me, that they may be one as we are one—²³I in them and you in me—so that they may be brought to complete unity. Then the world will know that you sent me and have loved them even as you have loved me."

John 10:30

> ³⁰I and the Father are one." *[Jesus' claim]*

Luke 8:18

Be aware! You are in a time of testing.

> [18]Therefore consider carefully how you listen. Whoever has will be given more; whoever does not have, even what they think they have will be taken from them.

Luke 8:12

> [12]Those along the path are the ones who hear, and then the devil comes and takes away the Word from their hearts, so that they may not believe and be saved.

Luke 8:13

> [13]Those on the rocky ground are the ones who receive the Word with joy when they hear it, but they have no root. They believe for a while, but in the time of testing they fall away.

Satan does have the power to steal the Word from your hearts! Here is proof that you can fall from grace:

Luke 8:12

I encourage you to be steadfast and not allow this to happen! For I believe that John 15:5 teaches that it is necessary to remain in the Word of God. I believe this scripture shows that even those once enlightened in God's Word can fall away from grace.

John 15:5

⁵I am the vine; you are the branches. If you remain in me and I in you, you will bear much fruit; apart from me you can do nothing.

Hebrews 6:4-6

⁴It is impossible for those who have once been enlightened, who have tasted the heavenly gift, who have shared in the Holy Spirit, ⁵who have tasted the goodness of the Word of God and the powers of the coming age ⁶and who have fallen away, to be brought back to repentance. To their loss they are crucifying the Son of God all over again and subjecting Him to public disgrace.

1 Peter 5:8

Be alert and of sober mind. Your enemy the devil prowls around like a roaring lion looking for someone to devour.

1 John 2:22

Who is the liar? It is whoever denies that Jesus is the Christ. Such a person is the antichrist—denying the Father and the Son.

2 John 1:7

I say this because many deceivers, who do not acknowledge Jesus Christ as coming in the flesh, have gone out into the world. Any such person is the deceiver and the antichrist.

2 Timothy 1:8

So, do not be ashamed of the testimony about our Lord or of me His prisoner. Rather, join with me in suffering for the Gospel, by the power of God.

Hebrews 13:6

So we say with confidence, "The Lord is my helper; I will not be afraid. What can mere mortals do to me?"

James 2:13

Because judgment without mercy will be shown to anyone who has not been merciful. Mercy triumphs over judgment.

Revelation 3:4

Yet you have a few people in Sardis who have not soiled their clothes. They will walk with me, dressed in white, for they are worthy.

WARNINGS:

1 Thessalonians 5:14

And we urge you, brothers and sisters, warn those who are idle and disruptive, encourage the disheartened, help the weak, be patient with everyone.

2 Thessalonians 3:6

> In the name of the Lord Jesus Christ, we command you, brothers and sisters, to keep away from every believer who is idle and disruptive and does not live according to the teaching you received from us. *[warning against idleness]*

2 Thessalonians 3:15

> Yet do not regard them as an enemy but warn them as you would a fellow believer.

1 Timothy 5:20

> But those elders who are sinning you are to reprove before everyone, so that the others may take warning.

2 Timothy 2:14

> Keep reminding God's people of these things. Warn them before God against quarreling about words; it is of no value, and only ruins those who listen. *[dealing with false teachers]*

Titus 3:10

> Warn a divisive person once, and then warn them a second time. After that, have nothing to do with them.

Hebrews 2:1

> We must pay the most careful attention, therefore, to what we have heard, so that we do not drift away. *[warning to pay attention]*

Hebrews 3:7

> So, as the Holy Spirit says: "Today, if you hear His voice" *[warning against unbelief]*

Hebrews 8:5

> They serve at a sanctuary that is a copy and shadow of what is in Heaven. This is why Moses was warned when he was about to build the tabernacle: "See to it that you make everything according to the pattern shown you on the mountain."

Hebrews 11:7

> By faith Noah, when warned about things not yet seen, in holy fear built an ark to save his family. By his faith he condemned the world and became heir of the righteousness that is in keeping with faith.

Hebrews 12:14

> Make every effort to live in peace with everyone and to be holy; without holiness no one will see the Lord. *[warning and encouragement]*

Hebrews 12:25

See to it that you do not refuse Him who speaks. If they did not escape when they refused Him who warned them on Earth, how much less will we, if we turn away from Him who warns us from Heaven?

1 John 2:18

Dear children, this is the last hour; and as you have heard that the antichrist is coming, even now many antichrists have come. This is how we know it is the last hour. *[warnings against denying the Son]*

Revelation 22:12

"Look, I am coming soon! My reward is with me, and I will give to each person according to what they have done." *[invitation and warning]*

Revelation 22:18

I warn everyone who hears the words of the prophecy of this scroll: If anyone adds anything to them, God will add to that person the plagues described in this scroll.

CHAPTER 18

WORKS REVEALED IN FIRE

1 Corinthians 3:10-15

2 Peter 3:10-15

> [10]But the day of the Lord will come like a thief. The heavens will disappear with a roar; the elements will be destroyed by fire, and the Earth and everything done in it will be laid bare. [11]Since everything will be destroyed in this way, what kind of people ought you to be? You ought to live holy and godly lives [12]as you look forward to the day of God and speed its coming. That day will bring about the destruction of the heavens by fire, and the elements will melt in the heat.

This is what is left after the fire!

- Those who share in the glory of God.
- The souls of men who are spiritually alive. (Those who do not have to bear the consequences of the second death, which is eternal punishment in the Lake of Fire.)
- Those who share in the Godhead Bodily.

- Those who are one with Christ, the Holy Spirit and God the Father—those who share in the resurrection.
- Those who together make up God's temple by putting on the character of Christ in baptism (Galatians 3:27).
- Those spiritual beings (workers), who have proven their faith by what they did (works) while on Earth in rightly handling the Word of Truth.
- True disciples of Christ will remain after the Great Fire and are those who are not ashamed to suffer as one who carries the name of Christ and glorify God in so doing.

1 Peter 4:16

> However, if you suffer as a Christian, do not be ashamed, but praise God that you bear that name.

Those who share in the blackness of darkness (the Abyss) with Satan and his angels.

The lost souls of those who did not accept the plan God has laid out for us (those who have to bear the consequences of the second death).

Luke 8:31

> And they begged Jesus repeatedly not to order them to go into the Abyss.

Revelation 9:1

> The fifth angel sounded his trumpet, and I saw a star that had fallen from the sky to the Earth. The star was given the key to the shaft of the Abyss.

Revelation 9:2

When He opened the Abyss, smoke rose from it like the smoke from a gigantic furnace. The sun and sky were darkened by the smoke from the Abyss.

Revelation 9:11

They had as king over them the angel of the Abyss, whose name in Hebrew is Abaddon and in Greek is Apollyon (that is, Destroyer).

Revelation 11:7

Now when they have finished their testimony, the beast that comes up from the Abyss will attack them and overpower and kill them.

Revelation 17:8

The beast, which you saw, once was, now is not, and yet will come up out of the Abyss and go to its destruction. The inhabitants of the Earth whose names have not been written in the Book of Life from the creation of the world will be astonished when they see the beast, because it once was, now is not, and yet will come.

Revelation 20:1

And I saw an angel coming down out of Heaven, having the key to the Abyss and holding in his hand a great chain. *[The Thousand Years]*

Revelation 20:3

> He threw him into the Abyss, and locked and sealed it over him, to keep him from deceiving the nations anymore until the thousand years were ended. After that, he must be set free for a short time.

Joel 2:2

> A day of darkness and gloom, a day of clouds and blackness. Like dawn spreading across the mountains a large and mighty army comes, such as never was in ancient times nor ever will be in ages to come.

Zephaniah 1:15

> That day will be a day of wrath— a day of distress and anguish, a day of trouble and ruin, a day of darkness and gloom, a day of clouds and blackness,

Jude 1

> [1]Jude, a servant of Jesus Christ and a brother of James, to those who have been called, who are loved in God the Father and kept for Jesus Christ: [2]Mercy, peace and love be yours in abundance.

The sin and doom of ungodly people:

> [3]Dear friends, although I was very eager to write to you about the salvation we share, I felt compelled to write and urge you to contend for the faith that was once for all entrusted to God's holy people. [4]For certain individuals whose condemnation was

written about long ago have secretly slipped in among you. They are ungodly people, who pervert the grace of our God into a license for immorality and deny Jesus Christ our only Sovereign and Lord.

⁵Though you already know all this, I want to remind you that the Lord at one time delivered His people out of Egypt, but later destroyed those who did not believe. ⁶And the angels who did not keep their positions of authority but abandoned their proper dwelling—these He has kept in darkness, bound with everlasting chains for judgment on the great Day. ⁷In a similar way, Sodom and Gomorrah and the surrounding towns gave themselves up to sexual immorality and perversion. They serve as an example of those who suffer the punishment of eternal fire.

⁸In the very same way, on the strength of their dreams these ungodly people pollute their own bodies, reject authority and heap abuse on celestial beings. ⁹But even the archangel Michael, when he was disputing with the devil about the Body of Moses, did not himself dare to condemn him for slander but said, "The Lord rebuke you!" ¹⁰Yet these people slander whatever they do not understand, and the very things they do understand by instinct—as irrational animals do—will destroy them.

¹¹Woe to them! They have taken the way of Cain; they have rushed for profit into Balaam's error; they have been destroyed in Korah's rebellion.

¹²These people are blemishes at your love feasts, eating with you without the slightest qualm—shepherds

who feed only themselves. They are clouds without rain, blown along by the wind; autumn trees, without fruit and uprooted—twice dead. [13]They are wild waves of the sea, foaming up their shame; wandering stars, for whom blackest darkness has been reserved forever.

[14]Enoch, the seventh from Adam, prophesied about them: "See, the Lord is coming with thousands upon thousands of His holy ones [15]to judge everyone, and to convict all of them of all the ungodly acts they have committed in their ungodliness, and of all the defiant words ungodly sinners have spoken against Him." [16]These people are grumblers and faultfinders; they follow their own evil desires; they boast about themselves and flatter others for their own advantage.

A call to persevere:

[17]But, dear friends, remember what the apostles of our Lord Jesus Christ foretold. [18]They said to you, "In the last times there will be scoffers who will follow their own ungodly desires." [19]These are the people who divide you, who follow mere natural instincts and do not have the Spirit.

[20]But you, dear friends, by building yourselves up in your most holy faith and praying in the Holy Spirit, [21]keep yourselves in God's love as you wait for the mercy of our Lord Jesus Christ to bring you to eternal life.

[22]Be merciful to those who doubt; [23]save others by snatching them from the fire; to others show mercy,

mixed with fear—hating even the clothing stained by corrupted flesh.

Doxology:

²⁴To him who can keep you from stumbling and to present you before His glorious presence without fault and with great joy— ²⁵to the only God our Savior be glory, majesty, power and authority, through Jesus Christ our Lord, before all ages, now and forevermore! Amen.

2 Timothy 2:15

Do your best to present yourself to God as one approved, a worker who does not need to be ashamed and who correctly handles the Word of Truth.

What pattern of teaching do I allow to claim my allegiance?

Romans 6

Dead to sin, alive in Christ:

What shall we say, then? Shall we go on sinning so that grace may increase? ²By no means! We are those who have died to sin; how can we live in it any longer? ³Or don't you know that all of us who were baptized into Christ Jesus were baptized into His death? ⁴We were therefore buried with Him through baptism into death in order that, just as Christ was raised from the dead through the glory of the Father, we too may live a new life.

⁵For if we have been united with Him in a death like His, we will certainly also be united with Him in a resurrection like His. ⁶For we know that our old self was crucified with Him so that the body ruled by sin might be done away with, that we should no longer be slaves to sin— ⁷because anyone who has died has been set free from sin.

⁸Now if we died with Christ, we believe that we will also live with Him. ⁹For we know that since Christ was raised from the dead, He cannot die again; death no longer has mastery over Him. ¹⁰The death He died, He died to sin once for all; but the life He lives, He lives to God.

¹¹In the same way, count yourselves dead to sin but alive to God in Christ Jesus. ¹²Therefore do not let sin reign in your mortal body so that you obey its evil desires. ¹³Do not offer any part of yourself to sin as an instrument of wickedness, but rather offer yourselves to God as those who have been brought from death to life; and offer every part of yourself to Him as an instrument of righteousness. ¹⁴For sin shall no longer be your master, because you are not under the law, but under grace.

Slaves to righteousness:

¹⁵What then? Shall we sin because we are not under the law but under grace? By no means! ¹⁶Don't you know that when you offer yourselves to someone as obedient slaves, you are slaves of the one you obey— whether you are slaves to sin, which leads to death, or to obedience, which leads to righteousness? ¹⁷But thanks be to God that, though you used to be slaves

to sin, you have come to obey from your heart the pattern of teaching that has now claimed your allegiance. [18]You have been set free from sin and have become slaves to righteousness.

[19]I am using an example from everyday life because of your human limitations. Just as you used to offer yourselves as slaves to impurity and to ever-increasing wickedness, so now offer yourselves as slaves to righteousness leading to holiness. [20]When you were slaves to sin, you were free from the control of righteousness. [21]What benefit did you reap at that time from the things you are now ashamed of? Those things result in death! [22]But now that you have been set free from sin and have become slaves of God, the benefit you reap leads to holiness, and the result is eternal life. [23]For the wages of sin is death, but the gift of God is eternal life in[b] Christ Jesus our Lord.

John 14:17

Even the Spirit of Truth; whom the world cannot receive, because it seeth Him not, neither knoweth Him: but ye know Him; for He dwelleth with you and shall be in you.

John 16:24

Hitherto have ye asked nothing in my name: ask, and ye shall receive, that your joy may be full.

Acts 1:8

But ye shall receive power, after that the Holy Ghost is come upon you: and ye shall be witnesses unto me both in Jerusalem, and in all Judaea, and in Samaria, and unto the uttermost part of the Earth.

Acts 2:38

Then Peter said unto them, repent, and be baptized every one of you in the name of Jesus Christ for the remission of sins, and ye shall receive the gift of the Holy Ghost.

Philippians 4:9

Those things, which ye have both learned, and received, and heard, and seen in me, do: and the God of peace shall be with you.

How to receive the reward of the inheritance into the Kingdom of Heaven:

Colossians 3:24

Knowing that of the Lord ye shall receive the reward of the inheritance: for ye serve the Lord Christ.

1 Peter 5:4

And when the chief Shepherd shall appear, ye shall receive a crown of glory that fadeth not away.

1 John 2:27

But the anointing which ye have received of Him abideth in you, and ye need not that any man teaches you: but as the same anointing teacheth you of all things, and is truth, and is no lie, and even as it hath taught you, ye shall abide in Him.

Revelation 2:11

He that hath an ear, let him hear what the Spirit saith unto the churches; he that overcometh shall not be hurt of the second death.

Revelation 20:6

Blessed and holy is He that hath part in the first resurrection: on such the second death hath no power, but they shall be priests of God and of Christ and shall reign with Him a thousand years.

How not to receive the reward of the inheritance into the Kingdom of Heaven:

Revelation 21:8

But the fearful, and unbelieving, and the abominable, and murderers, and whoremongers, and sorcerers, and idolaters, and all liars, shall have their part in the lake which burneth with fire and brimstone: which is the second death.

Revelation 20:10-15

[10]And the devil that deceived them was cast into the Lake of Fire and brimstone, where the beast and the false prophet are, and shall be tormented day and night for ever and ever. [11]And I saw a great white throne, and him that sat on it, from whose face the earth and heaven fled away; and there was

found no place for them. ¹²And I saw the dead, small and great, stand before God; and the books were opened: and another book was opened, which is the Book of Life: and the dead were judged out of those things which were written in the books, according to their works. ¹³And the sea gave up the dead which were in it; and death and hell delivered up the dead which were in them: and they were judged every man according to their works. ¹⁴And death and hell were cast into the Lake of Fire. This is the second death. ¹⁵And whosoever was not found written in the Book of Life was cast into the Lake of Fire.

2 Thessalonians 1:9

They will be punished with everlasting destruction and shut out from the presence of the Lord and from the glory of His might.

The importance of believing what I have just read:

Jesus put it this way in **John 14:**

> ²¹*Whoever has my commands and keeps them is the one who loves me. The one who loves me will be loved by my Father, and I too will love them and show myself to them."* ²²*Then Judas (not Judas Iscariot) said, "But, Lord, why do you intend to show yourself to us and not to the world?"* ²³*Jesus replied, "Anyone who loves me will obey my teaching. My Father will love them, and we will come to them and make our home with them.* ²⁴*Anyone who does not love me will not obey my teaching. These words you hear are not my own; they belong to the Father who sent me.* ²⁵*"All*

> *this I have spoken while still with you. *²⁶*But the Advocate, the Holy Spirit, whom the Father will send in my name, will teach you all things and will remind you of everything I have said to you. *²⁷*Peace I leave with you; my peace I give you. I do not give to you as the world gives. Do not let your hearts be troubled and do not be afraid."*

Some may ask, why do you spend your time putting this information in a book? The Bible has it all. Very simply, I work in the ROK, an environment in which many times having offered a Bible to co-workers, they will not even accept it. This is my attempt to get the Word of God into their hands as I spend 7 months each year in their country. I see and live in the oppression which is propagated into their culture. I cannot think of another way to get the truth into their hands. It is a sad situation for sure.

There is a pattern of sound words in the Bible to hold on to in love and faith. There are many other promises and facts in the Bible which I have not addressed. It is my hope that when you need answers, or just need a message to give someone who is in despair, you can now give a reason for hope within this book. I leave you with these three admonitions:

Romans 12:9

> **Let love be without dissimulation. Abhor that which is evil; cleave to that which is good.**

James 4:7

> **Submit yourselves therefore to God. Resist the devil, and he will flee from you.**

Steve C. Varner

<u>Philippians 3:10</u>

I want to know Christ—yes, to know the power of his resurrection and participation in his sufferings, becoming like him in his death,

In Christian Love,
A brother in Christ

Printed in the United States
By Bookmasters